WHERE'S THE DUCK IN PEKING?

Glimpses of China

Cliff Schimmels

Foreword by
Daryl McCarthy

Cooperative Studies Publishing Co.
Overland Park KS

Where's the Duck in Peking?
Glimpses of China
Cliff Schimmels

Published by Cooperative Studies Publishing Co., PO Box 12830, Overland Park KS
66282-2830. Phone number 913-962-9961. www.coopstudies.org

ISBN 0-9705932-0-1

Cover design and illustration © 2000 by David Nelson
Typesetting by Prof. Paul Mouw, Judson College, Judson, Illinois
Printed in the United States of America.

ƀ

Publisher's Cataloging-in-Publication
(Provided by Quality Books, Inc.)

Schimmels, Cliff
   Where's the duck in Peking? : glimpses of China /
Cliff Schimmels ; foreword by Daryl McCarthy. -- 1st ed.
   p. cm.
   ISBN: 0-9705932-0-1

   1. China--Description and travel. 2. Schimmels,
Cliff--Journeys--China.   I. Title.

DS712.S35 2001   951.05'9
                                 QBI01-200809

Table of Contents

C

Contents

Other books by Cliff Schimmels

Oh No! Maybe My Child is Normal!
And Then There Were Two: Empty Nesting After Your Kids Fly the Coop
Teaching That Works
Lessons From The Good Old Days
What Parents Try to Forget About Adolescence
Other People My Age Are Already Grown Up
T-Shirt Wisdom
All I Really Need to Know I Learned in Sunday School
The Middle School Maze
How to Survive and Thrive in College
How to Help Your Child Survive and Thrive in Public School
The Last-Minute Sunday School Teacher
Questions Parents Ask About Kids in School
Rites of Autumn—The Wheatheart Chronicles
Winter Hunger—The Wheatheart Chronicles
Rivals of Spring—The Wheatheart Chronicles
How to Shape Your Child's Education

Foreword

by Dr. Daryl McCarthy

"We will be the super-power of this century!" Everywhere you go in China, people are talking about the new prominence of their nation in the world community. It fills young people with pride to think that their nation will be a major force in the world and they are a part of this manifest destiny! The national psyche of China has changed dramatically in the past twenty years. In the last century, the Chinese people have gone from an introverted satisfaction with their own history and accomplishments, to comparison with the rest of the world, to a sense of inferiority and now, in the last decade, pride as they compare themselves with the rest of the world. They are determined to be the biggest and the best in the world.

When Mao Tse-tung stood at Tiananmen Square on Oct 1, 1949, after the victory of the Communists in the 50-year struggle to control China, he declared, "Today, the Chinese people have stood up." Now more than fifty years later, the Chinese are standing up again—taller than ever.

Today China is undergoing the most profound and far-reaching revolution in its 6000-year history. No other nation in history has enjoyed a greater increase in the personal income of its citizens, in a shorter period of time, than the Chinese have experienced in the last ten years. This economic development has been made possible by a significant political shift. The economic and political changes are in turn causing major cultural, social and ethical changes—and dilemmas—for the nation and its people. China is experiencing a revolution of historic proportions at every level of life and society. The world is watching a new China emerge, a China very different from the China of old.

The historian Arnold Toynbee predicted that the twenty-first century would be China's century. Now it is clear that Toynbee spoke prophetically. Most Westerners have forgotten that for most of the centuries preceding the 1500's, China was the most advanced civilization on earth. But in more recent centuries, it has been a divided and declining civilization—that is, until the late twentieth century. Now the "Middle Kingdom" (the meaning of China's name in Mandarin, or "the center of the universe") is moving front and center on the world stage.

UNIVERSITIES AND THE FUTURE OF CHINA

"China's strategy to achieve their goal of being the world superpower begins with education." This is how my wife, Teri, explains why work in China's universities is so important. Teri has been teaching and consulting with Chinese universities since the early 1980's and has watched this hunger for recognition from the rest of the world grow dramatically, until now it is a prominent feature of the national self-consciousness as well as the stated agenda of the political and military systems of China.

With one of the largest university systems in the world, China has an estimated six million college students. Yet this is only seven percent of the college-age population (*Chronicle of Higher Education*, XLVI (35), A54-55). So you are truly teaching the cream of the crop when you teach in a Chinese university.

Historian Jaroslav Pelikan of Yale said, "The university is a staging area for the future...." (*The Idea of a University* (New Haven: Yale University Press, 1992), 148). Truly the universities of China are the preparatory stage for the country's future. The ideas and philosophies taught there will shape the next generations of the world's largest nation. Universities are key in determining the direction of a civilization, and especially a civilization going through as much dramatic and rapid change as the China of today.

Many Chinese know there is a struggle for the soul of their culture. One Chinese educator declared, "China is in moral confusion." The economic and social revolution in China is bringing a disintegration of traditional Chinese values. The Chinese tradition has long exalted the person of honor. With 5,000 years of history there is a deeply ingrained code of ethics and commitment to the community. Even during the last fifty years of Communism, a high standard of public morality was upheld, including such values as sexual chastity, a prohibition on drug abuse and homosexuality and service for the community and others.

Many forms of traditionally-prohibited behavior are sweeping across China—materialism, which was long scorned by both traditional Chinese and by Chinese Communist ideals; illicit sexual conduct which has been outlawed and punishable for centuries, and other vices. Chinese culture was built on an others-centered mentality. Now Western capitalism, devoid of its historic Judeo-Christian underpinnings, is spawning a movement of self-centeredness, egotism and self-aggrandizement. And the elders are shaking their heads in amazement at what the young people are becoming. Their own dear young people are more concerned about themselves than about their family, their village or their nation.

Even many thoughtful young people are disconcerted. After I lectured graduate philosophy students at Hangzhou University, one bright student stood and asked, "In America many students have much money and use drugs and have babies before they are married. Now in China we are facing a similar situation. What should be our attitude about money? Are we to worship it?" But earlier in the class, another student had posed the question, "Does not truth apply only to scientific matters and not to values and ethics?" The doctrine of ethical relativism is now being promoted in Chinese universities.

A little more than a decade ago, selfless young Chinese students were prepared to die for their commitment to their ideals—and many did. But now few Chinese students are willing to die for anything, because they are too busy living for themselves. What a change in ten years!

COOPERATIVE STUDIES IN CHINA

This change is why China and other nations in Asia are asking the West for teachers with integrity and character. It is only natural that Chinese government leaders and university officials respond with open arms to Cooperative Studies (CS). We are able to assure these officials, "We know that sometimes you have been offended and hurt by Westerners coming here as mavericks, who are immoral and dishonest and flaunt their disregard for Chinese morality. That is why we will screen all the professors we send you very carefully. We will insure that they have high academic standards, that they are good communicators in the classroom, that they love students, that they are good listeners, that they are good learners. But we will also try to make sure that they are persons of high moral and ethical character, that they are honest and upright, that they keep their word and their commitments and that they honor traditional Chinese values. We will do our best to send you men and women of integrity and character." (See Appendix B for more information about teaching opportunities with Cooperative Studies.)

Cooperative Studies and its affiliates have been establishing partnerships with universities in China since 1991 when our first protocol with Peking University was signed. In October 1994, along with Peking University, we co-sponsored the first Symposium of Chinese-American Philosophy and Religious Studies. This historic symposium brought ten leading American philosophers of religion (including Al Plantinga (Notre Dame), Eleanor Stump (St. Louis University), Mel Stewart (Bethel), Linda Zagzebski (Loyola), Bill Hasker (Huntington College), Alan Padgett (Azusa Pacific University) George Mavrodes (University of Michigan) and Bill Alston (Syracuse University)) together with several of the top philosophy and religion scholars in China for three days of presentations of papers and discussion. The exchanges were spirited and lively as the Americans and Chinese struggled to understand and communicate with each other. But honest dialogue, joint publication projects and long-term friendships resulted.

Cooperative Studies is an international academic resource organization which primarily places professors in public universities outside of North America and the UK. The mission of CS is to serve as a conduit for resources, promoting cooperation throughout the higher education community around the world. Through a partnership designed uniquely for each university, Cooperative Studies provides professors to teach on university faculties for a semester or longer, sponsors special guest lectureships, provides books for the university library, establishes exchange programs and participates in consultation for academic programs and curriculum development. (See Appendix A for more information on how universities can develop partnerships with Cooperative Studies.)

CLIFF AND MARY SCHIMMELS ARRIVE IN CHINA

One of my favorite teachers is Dr. Cliff Schimmels. Cliff and I got acquainted in 1990. We began working together following his resignation after seventeen years of teaching at prestigious Wheaton College in Illinois. He accepted a teaching assignment with our organization in Kiev, Ukraine.

Since our first meeting Cliff has never ceased to be a source of both wisdom and laughter. Cliff has an uncanny ability to give perspective—a fresh, unique look at things, so I value his counsel and advice and his friendship.

That is why I was delighted when I learned that he was writing this book about one of my favorite countries in the world—China. Cliff is a great writer. With his own inimitable style, he makes his readers laugh on one page, cry on the next and ponder profound insights on the next. He has authored more than twenty books, including both non-fiction and fiction, since his first and ever-popular World's Oldest Freshman.

The book you are about to enjoy on China is written in the same easy-reading, but poignant style as the popular Where's the Chicken in Kiev?, which Dr. Schimmels wrote after serving for a year as a Distinguished Teaching Fellow in Ukraine in 1991 with our organization.

He readily admits that none of this would have been possible without Mary's unflagging energy, patience and wisdom. Mary assists him at Lee University and in traveling with him all over the world. They have been married for 42 years and are the proud parents of three children and four grandchildren.

Dr. Schimmels and his wife Mary have taught and lectured in many countries around the world. Most recently they have focused on China, with Cliff serving as a Distinguished Teaching Fellow with CS at Zheijiang Normal University in Jinhua, China. He is providing counsel and direction for an innovative curriculum reform project which is re-designing the way middle school foreign language teachers are taught in the Zhejiang Province.

Often as I lecture at Chinese universities I am overwhelmed by the eagerness, the impressionability of the students—these future leaders of China. That is why it is deeply gratifying to know that in some small way Cooperative Studies is helping this great nation. Hopefully, we are helping it to reach for goodness as well as greatness. Cliff and Mary Schimmels' presence in China has made a significant contribution.

China is one of the most fascinating nations in the world. And with this book, you will see why Cliff and Mary Schimmels love this country. You will get to know the people of China and their ways. You will glimpse their culture through the unique perspective of the Schimmels. Get ready to laugh, to cry, to ponder, to stretch your mind. Enjoy!

A Tribute to Clifford Dean Schimmels

1937-2001

by Dr. Daryl McCarthy

On May 9, 2001, as this book was in final preparation for publication, Dr. Cliff Schimmels passed away while undergoing medical tests in Chattanooga, Tennessee. (The autopsy revealed that his body had been devastated by a rare, incurable disease known as amyloidosis.) Though he had been ill for several months, his wide circle of family and friends around the globe were unprepared. But he was prepared. In the weeks preceding his death, Cliff had reflected with Mary and his children on how blessed he had been and that "if the Lord came back today, I am ready."

Cliff Schimmels was one of the smartest men I ever knew. He had a breadth of knowledge and a depth of intelligence that was astounding. Yet he was consistently underestimated because he hid his gifts so well under his truly humble, down-home, Oklahoma boy personality. The Chinese, with surprise, would say he was much wiser than he looked.

But Cliff was not only intelligent, he was wise. During the years we worked and traveled together, he never failed to provide sound counsel and valuable insight, whether it was a question on how to raise my kids, how to deal with a personnel problem or how to manage an organization.

Cliff Schimmels was one of the funniest men I have ever known. He could be funny without even trying to be, though I wasn't always sure whether he was trying or not. Some people's humor is at the expense of others. His humor was usually at his own expense and never failed to reach out to others. Cliff once counseled one of my colleagues on how to deal with problems, "If you are going to laugh about it in ten years, go ahead and laugh about it now."

Cliff was a master communicator — both in writing and speaking. He was internationally recognized as a master teacher — the best of the best. And he was a classic teacher of teachers. One couldn't always explain his impact. It was often beyond analysis. But with one story, or sometimes with one line, he could make a point that it would take others an hour to make.

He was an award-winning and prodigious (a word Cliff would never use) writer, producing more than 30 books. He wrote with an ease and flair that few authors ever gain. Much of the secret of his genius as a teacher and writer was that he was a master storyteller. People the world over loved his stories. He took you there — whether to the little towns of western Oklahoma where he spent his early years, to the classrooms of Wheaton College and Lee University where he taught for more than 27 years, to the high school where he became "the world's oldest freshman," to an Orthodox cathedral in Ukraine, or talking to students at a university campus in China — you were there with him.

Like another famous Oklahoman, Will Rogers, Cliff Schimmels loved people. He was devoted to his family above all — Mary and his children, Chris, Paula and Larry and their families. Cliff was a great friend. The morning before his funeral, it hit me — I had just lost one of my very best friends. When we walked into the Freewill Baptist Church in Clinton, Oklahoma on Mother's Day afternoon, May 13, we were greeted by Russell Rayner. As Russell visited with my wife Teri and me, he said, "Clifford and I went to school together from first grade, right on up through all the grades. Clifford — he was my best friend." At that moment

I realized there were hundreds of people around the world saying, "Cliff Schimmels was one of my best friends."

Cliff always had time to visit whether with colleagues, young people, students, children or relatives. He was always available to encourage, to challenge, to inspire. He was genuinely interested, honestly concerned about others. Hardly a conversation would end without him asking about my children who loved him dearly and his offering to help them in some way. Cliff was transparent. There was no hypocrisy, no false fronts. He had a talent for expressing tough truth with a loving bluntness, often launching into a surprise conversation with, "You're not going to like this, but..." Then he would surprise with an angle you had never thought of and winsomely convince you of his point.

Cliff was generous. He and Mary invested in scores of students' lives at Wheaton and Lee through their hospitality and assistance. In days when we were struggling financially, they often traveled and spoke for our organization, sometimes getting expenses covered, sometimes not even that, because they believed heart and soul in what we were doing — placing Christian professors in public universities around the world. He and Mary generously sponsored individuals from Ukraine and China to come to the US for medical care or for education.

Cliff was also a risk-taker. Although he could have basked in the safety of his reputation and the campuses of Wheaton and Lee, he ventured out to teach for Cooperative Studies in Kiev, Ukraine in 1991, when the dangers from Chernobyl — just 90 miles away — were still very real. In 1998, he again went to teach for Cooperative Studies in Jinhua, China, a six-hour train ride south of Shanghai. Although he was royally received, Jinhua was not an easy place for a Westerner to live. He knew the risks, but he went anyway.

Cliff finished the race. As a former football coach and marathon runner, Cliff practiced perseverance. He didn't give up. In the spring of 1999, Teri and I visited him and Mary in Jinhua. He was down, discouraged, which was very unusual for his upbeat personality. But he didn't stop. He kept right on teaching, right on meeting with scores of teachers and students, right on speaking at special events across the Zheijiang Province. In spite of his discouragement, in spite of intense pain in his knees, Cliff Schimmels kept right on walking and talking all over the globe, wearing out three passports on the way.

Finally, Cliff Schimmels was a World Christian who took seriously his privilege to share the love of Christ with people around the world. He was willing to take breaks in his career and to lose out on many well-paying speaking engagements to spend and be spent overseas, in difficult, obscure places. In the process he mobilized scores of students and faculty in North America, giving them a vision for educational service overseas.

As he poured himself out, lives were forever changed. He often remembered Maria, a Ukrainian faculty member with whom the Schimmels' taught at Kiev State Linguistic University. Maria co-authored Cliff's book on his experiences as a Cooperative Studies professor in Ukraine entitled, Where's the Chicken in Kiev? A few months later, she became very ill with leukemia caused by fallout from Chernobyl. Cliff and Mary brought her to the US for treatments, but it was too late. She returned to Ukraine to die. Cliff didn't often cry, but with tears in his eyes, he would reflect on their time in Ukraine, "All the difficulties, all the days we couldn't communicate, all the nights we had no shower, all the bone-jarring travel on dirty trains — it was all worth it. Maria is in heaven today, because we went to Ukraine."

A few days before his death, Teri and I called Cliff. That day we insisted that he hear us out as we expressed our deep love and appreciation for him, especially in setting out a plan for Teri's recently-completed Ph.D. dissertation. But he kept insisting that we were overstating his help and his role in our lives. If he heard this tribute and all the others which have been uttered since his death, Cliff would wave away all this talk about himself and with his characteristic disarming humility, insist, "Wait a minute, you guys. You are really putting the emphasis in the wrong place." Pointing to Jesus is the greatest legacy of Cliff Schimmels.

Introduction

In August of 1998, Mary and I went to China to teach, but we cheated. Instead of being teachers, we became learners.

Our friends, Dr. Daryl McCarthy, head of Cooperative Studies, and his wife, Teri McCarthy, Communications Director of CS, had talked to us about an opportunity they had uncovered during a trip to the Orient. They had found a spot for two Christian teachers to spend a year at the expense of the university. We thought that sounded like a win-win situation, so after persuading Dr. Conn, Dr. Murray, and the other good people at Lee University to give us a year off, we signed up for an exciting new venture.

Teachers – English teachers at Zhejiang Normal University, Jinhua, People's Republic of China from August 28, 1998, until July 4, 1999. That's what our visas said we were supposed to do.

And we did it. We taught classes almost every day. On the campus of eight thousand wannabe teachers, six hundred of them are English majors. Mary taught the first-year students of that category in weekly lessons of conversational English. I taught the second-year students English composition and survey of America.

We prepared our lessons; we gathered our materials; we clothed ourselves in our best teacher emotions; we went to class and we learned. Every day we learned!

This book is our record of what we learned. The logical way to organize our experiences would be to pick a theme and develop it historically, sociologically, philosophically and culturally. This structure would provide us with tidy chapters which would meet the Aristotelian principle of unity, time, place and action. Or at least it would give us chapters with a beginning, middle and conclusion. That would make a good book – a scholarly tome – a comprehensive and scientific analysis of the Chinese mind and culture.

But we didn't write that book for one simple reason: we don't know how. After living in China for almost a year, we don't have the stuff. We tried. We tried to analyze. We tried to back off, to stand at a distance, observe, record, analyze, categorize and comprehend. But we failed. The more we tried our scientific analysis of China, the more confused we became.

China is too vibrant, too big, too populated, too historically rooted, too modernistically dynamic and too complex.

Maybe we were too busy ourselves, wrapped up in teaching and living to stand back. The impressions tumbled across our points of reference in such great number and in such disarray that we never managed to put any of them into neat packages.

Thus, we present our experiences as they flitted across our horizons: glimpses, or in contemporary parlance - sound bytes from China.

If you have the kind of mind that demands structure, feel free to search for such things as themes and rhythms in our pages, but just remember that we didn't intend any. In the meantime, read the book for the purpose in which we wrote it and the reason we went to China: to fall in love with a billion of God's people and to stand in open mouthed-wonder at the complexity of their heritage.

Four to One

People! The distinguishing characteristic of China is people. The ancient temples are provocative. The Great Wall is inspiring. The Himalayas are beautiful. The trains are interesting. But the sharp characteristic – the one that grabs you first and stays with you throughout your stay - is the almost indescribable and incomprehensible volume of people. Everywhere, people!

Statistics? 1.4 billion! But what does it all mean? Just a lot of people? No, it's much more than that. Try multiplying by four. How many vehicles pass through the green light? Twenty? No, eighty! How many people stand in line at the tourist trap? One hundred? No, four hundred! How many students in the second grade class? Twenty? No, eighty! How many girls in a college dormitory room? Two? No, eight! How many students apply for admission to study for a degree? Five hundred? No, two thousand! How many people sit down to supper every night? Two hundred and seventy million? No, 1.4 billion!

When we think of China in any context — business opportunities, comparable military strength, social policy, institutions, exchange programs, and evangelical opportunities — we have to ground our thinking on the phenomenon of the volume of people. It is difficult to understand anything about China until we understand that fact.

Statistics? 1.4 billion – just another number. But when you get past the teeming hordes in the streets, when you get past the crowds in the shops, when you get past the shoulder-to-shoulder jostling on the buses, when you get past the thousands of workers working side-by-side digging a ditch or building a road, when you get past the sense of the multitude, you will find that each one of those 1.4 billion people is a person created by God in the image of God, badly in need of a Savior.

4

Local Talk

Trivia question: what language is spoken in the People's Republic of China? Mandarin? That's what I would have answered. Surprise! They call it something else. But that's a different story. The answer to the original question is: there is no answer.

The Chinese speak a local language. In other words, every village has its own language. We're not just talking dialect with unusual pronunciations here; we're talking language! Different vocabulary! Different tones! Different grammar! From village to village! Literally thousands of languages!

Of course, there is an official language, the language of Beijing which the Chinese call Putonghua. This is the written language, the formal language, and the language of business and government. Most children first meet this language when they start to school because it is also the language of education. This universal bilingualism presents an interesting twist. Most people speak one language at home and in the neighborhood and another in school and business transactions.

Those who don't get out much or get much formal education are obviously limited to fluency in the local language only. They can't go shopping in the neighboring village; they can't travel on the trains; they can't visit with strangers in their own village.

This does present some frustration to our university students. For one thing, those from the more traditional families living in the more traditional communities come to university with some gaps in their ability to handle Putonghua. Thus, they have to take remedial courses in speaking their own language. This is rather embarrassing.

The students also have problems shopping with the local merchants. Graciously, some of our students volunteered to help us buy necessities, particularly from the street vendors who were selling local fruits and vegetables. Our students were afraid that our inexperience would open the gate to the merchants to take advantage of us. But when we started to make the deal, the local merchants refused to speak any language except the Jinhua dialect. This frustrated the students. They would shout in their best Putonghua. The merchants shouted back. Rather than getting fresh oranges, we got a lesson in how Chinese argue in languages neither contestant understands.

In the midst of this language confusion, many of the students live their university life with the image of a grandmother back home always looking over their shoulders. Very few of our students, among the finest in all of China, could ever dream of going anywhere after graduation except back to their home-towns. For awhile I didn't understand that. Why not dream of Shanghai or Beijing or some of the other romantic spots? Although this question doesn't have one simple answer, one of the reasons our students want to go home again is that they know the language.

The other caution for our students was dating and the universal university activity of spousal search. Many of our students were very reluctant to allow themselves to entertain any thoughts of mingling with classmates of the opposite sex. They justified this by saying that such activity would affect their study, but I suspect another reason. When they left to come all the way to Jinhua to spend four years of their lives, their grandmothers assured them of the virtue of marrying someone who can speak their local language. How else could she give her approval?

Our friend puts the whole issue in perspective for us. Moving to Jinhua from another city, she can speak her native language, but she can't speak to her neighbors. Her husband is from yet another city, and neither can have a conversation with in-laws. However, the high school son has mastered the language of both sets of grandparents as well as the Jinhua language. They call him the Interpreter!

7

Bicycles

Bicycle traffic jams, bicycle parking problems, bicycle reckless driving citations, bicycle repair shops, no minimum age for bicycle riders.

China is a bicycle culture. That is more than a comment about machines. It is also a statement about sociological analysis.

One of the first impressions of the place is the sheer quantity of bicycles everywhere. Try imagining a billion people. Now try imagining a billion people riding a bicycle to work. That's a lot of bicycles — all sorts of bicycles, too. There are single passenger bicycles, bicycles built to carry loads such as gas bottles or water jars and family-oriented bicycles with a baby seat on the front fender and a place for Mom to ride sidesaddle on the back. There are even pick-up truck bicycles for farmers and merchants and other small business people. These are actually tricycles equipped with three wheels and a box large enough to carry a few bushels of grain or some produce to the market. In other words, China is a nation on wheels — bicycle wheels.

As something of an uncoordinated mess myself, I was impressed with the dexterity of the riders. They are good, balancing a sidesaddle rider or carrying a load on only one side. They themselves go riding down the street so nonchalantly that I realized that this is something enmeshed in the culture.

I was also impressed with the problems caused by the bicycles. Students would come running to class almost late because they couldn't find a place to park their bikes. Several students, who either forgot the rules or were showing signs of rebellion, parked their bicycles near the fire hydrant at the library. Security came with one of those pick-up truck machines and towed them all away. One of the students was injured when two bicycles collided at a blind intersection — all the problems we encounter with the car.

Someday when I have the time to sit under a cottonwood tree on a creek bank somewhere, I am going to ponder the sociological implications of a bicycle culture. The logical explanation is volume. If that many people had cars, what problems we would see!

But there is more to ponder – the physical grace to master bicycle riding, the proximity of people on bicycles not surrounded by a mass of steel, the sheer functionality of a machine capable of carrying one into small spaces.

Or maybe it's just another method of getting to work.

10

Inherent Goodness

"The difference between China and the West is religious and philosophical," Mr. Gu told the students gathered in the lecture hall. "Western Christianity is based on original sin. On the other hand, we Chinese believe in the inherent goodness of people."

Mr. Gu is an insightful man. In addition to being the foreign affairs director with an opportunity to travel, to visit with foreigners, and to master conversational English, he is a philosopher. Educated in translation theory, he has studied the writings of Western philosophers.

His observation about the philosophical difference between his culture and mine merits my attention and my pondering.

There were occasions when I thought I might have spotted some results of the stated philosophy. Although child rearing is child rearing regardless of where you are, there are some subtle differences. The Chinese don't put diapers on their children. Instead, they give the children the convenience of pants with a slit — just one example of a little less social restriction on an infant, but maybe it does serve as a symbol of an underlying philosophy.

Some parents did carry this freedom concept a bit further, giving their young children opportunities to run, explore, examine, and bang. It was interesting to note that mothers seemed quite comfortable to watch the child playing unrestrictedly, but grandparents seemed to be a little uneasy with all that free expression.

Other than that, I had difficulty in seeing many examples of the inherent goodness philosophy in practice. Students and teachers live with mandates and laws. Authorities inspect dormitory rooms, conduct bed checks, monitor examinations, demand doctor excuses for absences, and generally act as if every person is capable of taking advantage of the situation. Shoppers don't trust the merchants; passengers don't trust the cab drivers; and the first three floors of apartment buildings come equipped with bars on the windows to discourage the thieves.

Despite all this, the idea of inherent goodness merits our thoughts. As we continue to interact with the Chinese in business, cultural exchange, and ministry, we need to be aware of how this tenet in the national ethos plays a role in our relationship.

Arthur, Water, Bowl and the Other Girls

All students study English from the seventh grade throughout the rest of their formal education. Most students have an interesting love-hate relationship with the language. Those who love it more than they hate it decide that somewhere during the process, they should have an English name.

With the aid of a dictionary, a Charles Dickens novel, a textbook, or the counsel of a foreign friend (teacher or fellow student), they select from a varied menu and give themselves their cherished English identity.

Some English names are actually rather appropriate because they sound much like the person's Chinese name. Some thoughtful person at least saw some similarity and chose accordingly. That's why you find many Leigh Anns in the group.

Most Chinese names have a specific meaning in the language; so, often, that meaning is translated into the nearest English concept. That's why our good friend has the name of Hope and her friend is named Moonlight.

Other than that, the guiding principle of choosing the appropriate English identity is whether the student likes the sound of the word. Of course, the whole process is skewed by such circumstances as which novel they have just finished reading or from what part of the English speaking world this year's foreign teacher happens to be. If the teacher is from Scotland, we get Fionas. If the teacher is from the Deep South in the United States, we get Mary Lous and Elizabeth Sues.

Actually, one of the surprises about accepting an opportunity to be the foreign English teacher in China is to encounter suddenly the power of naming 125 children. No wonder some girls are Arthur and some girls are Bowl.

For some Chinese students, those English names take on significance. If they become English teachers or they travel to the West, they become identified with a name that was assigned to them in a rather nonchalant fashion. As foreign teachers, we used our students' English names in all of our relationships with them; but we always did it with a certain amount of guilt because, surely, people would prefer to be identified by the name their parents gave them rather than some other name even if they picked it themselves.

Slippers

One of the symbols of Chinese gentility is waiting for you right at the door – slippers! When you come into a person's home, your first step is to stop at the stoop and take off your shoes, removing the dirt and the bustle of the outside world. Then you wrap your feet into the comforting sensation of a toasty pair of slippers so that your presence in the home and your conversation can be warm and comfortable.

Of course it is all for a very practical reason. The streets and the paths you walked across to get to this place were full of trash – items of trash which we won't enumerate here – garbage of the worst degree.

You don't want to track that into anyone's home, so you change shoes at the door. Sure, it's for a very practical reason, but it's also so gentle and so gracious, and the slippers are themselves wonderful, coming in great variety – leather slippers which suggest comfortable authority, fuzzy slippers which suggest embraces and warmth, cloth slippers which suggest relaxation and ease.

A reminder of the distance between the private life and public life! A symbol of the devotion to home and family! A gesture of friendship!

When company comes to our house in Tennessee, we greet them warmly and ask them to remove their coats so that we can all be friendly and comfortable.

When company comes to our house in China, we offer them slippers.

Rice, Noodles
or Dumplings

"Could you join us at the restaurant for supper?"

"Sure," we agreed, knowing that we would be in for some surprises, but we're not novices just off the turnip truck.

We were wise enough to pace ourselves – through twenty-one courses we paced ourselves. Through the dishes of vegetables of variety, meats, tofu, all specialties and tasty, we paced ourselves. Through two hours of conversation and whirling the lazy Susan around and around, we paced ourselves.

When we hit a lull in the conversation and the nibbling and were just getting ready to rejoice in our achievement of resistance, they sprang the surprise. "Now, what do you want for the main course – rice, noodles or dumplings?"

We thought we had finished when all we had done was sample the appetizers.

China is a big country, and eating practices vary from region to region, but this was the ceremony for formal meals in our area. Regardless of how many preliminary dishes we might have devoured, we always finished with a substantial serving of rice, noodles, or dumplings. Either our Chinese hosts had larger appetites than we did or they paced better.

In the midst of all this, I remembered the words of my mother. "Eat that food on your plate. There are starving children in China who could live on your scraps."

My, how times have changed.

Classroom
Referees

When it came time to study the American political system, I decided to try a little innovation – a bit of a simulation. I don't know why I come up with such ideas. Projects are always a risk. You think up the creative approach. In your excitement you work out the plans and put them into motion.

That's when you make a commitment to the project. You spend the next week in total fear, imagining every possible catastrophe lurking to wreck your best laid plans, knowing full well that the whole thing will come crashing down in total failure, and you will be the laughing stock of the students and faculty alike. Why wasn't I content just to lecture in the old tried and boring method?

Instead we planned an election. I picked two guys to be Republican candidates for president and vice-president, and I picked two girls to be Democratic candidates.

In the meantime, we registered the other 125 students in the class, decorated a ballot box, and waited. Not patiently but with excruciating anxiety, I waited the required week until the next class.

Was I pleasantly surprised! As soon as I walked into the classroom, I realized that my fears were ungrounded. The whole place had been decorated with placards, banners, and slogans all promoting planks in the platform not unlike we would expect at the national conventions in the United States. We had parades and songs and demonstrations, but the crowning achievement was the speeches by the candidates themselves.

They had all gone to the library, studied old speeches by Richard Nixon and John Kennedy, and had built platforms very similar to party lines. I was impressed. No, I was overwhelmed – relieved and overwhelmed!

After we had finished the speeches, I designated students in the audience to represent the press and ask the candidates tough questions. Sam, a bright young man who is resourceful enough to stay current on American affairs, threw out an open and relevant question. "If you are elected, will you endorse a program of assisted suicide?"

Helen, the Democratic vice-presidential candidate (who incidentally looks like Pocahontas in the Disney movie) had been rather quiet throughout the festivity, playing the vice-presidential role well. But when she heard Sam's question, she came to life.

"Absolutely not!" she declared firmly. "There will be no program for assisted suicide, and also," she continued with fire, "there will be no legal abortion."

I gulped and caught my breath. Does she remember where we are? This is China, the home of the one child policy. Does she want to say this here?

Helen wasn't finished. "Life is a gift given to us by God, and only He can take it away – not the government." Students nodded in agreement.

I sat there and thought, "God, did you bring me all the way to China just to get an argument started?"

And He answered, "Yep."

Ringing
Pockets

The land of the Great Wall, The Summer Palace, Seven Dragons, and dynasties from thousands of years ago! Now, it's also the land of the cell phone! According to their news agencies, China is the second largest cell phone user in the world. I have no idea who the largest user is, but I can't imagine being anywhere with anymore ringing pockets. It seemed to me that everyone had one. On the trains, in the streets, in the shops, in the restaurants, in the taxis, at meetings – everywhere we went, people were using the cell phone.

I wasn't prepared for that little feature of Chinese culture. When we were there only ten years ago, the telephone was a mysterious luxury used only by the chosen few who had been trained in the art of telephoning because the equipment was less than state of the art technology. Most of the people we met then never had a phone number, never expected to have one, and had no idea they would ever be available to have access to a telephone, much less one in their pocket.

So the first point is progress – just another ringing reminder of how fast the country has moved – how the rites of modernity can rapidly flow into all streams of the population. To me this is the awesome reality – how very quickly conditions can change. Ten years ago I simply could not have believed it could happen. Progress just can't move that fast. There have to be prerequisite infrastructures, intermediate steps, and dialectic changes of bureaucracy. This all takes time – not a decade but at least a generation. But it did happen. I saw it with my own eyes. Not only is it a source of awe for me, but it is also a source of hope – a reason to believe.

Some experts use terms like first world and third world. I don't know what those mean, but those ringing pockets in China convince me that the chasm that separates countries could be bridged in just a short time – emphasize could be!

I can't explain why these symbols of progress are so rampant in China. Do the Chinese have a natural curiosity for technology? Is the phone progress somehow related to the economic progress? Do the Chinese, as a culture and a government, have a compelling need to move with the most technologically-advanced nations as a statement of national pride? Are they using the phone so much because it is something of a new toy? Maybe they just like talking to each other.

Tones and Word Choice

As a language learner, I call myself a survivalist. Every time I enter a country, I learn enough expressions to survive – four in fact. "Hello," "Goodbye," "Thank you," and "I can't speak your language."

That has always been my modus operandi, until I arrived in China. Even with those simple words, I learned a big lesson about Putonghua (the Chinese word for Mandarin), the official Chinese language. You don't speak it. You sing it.

Let me explain. All languages that I had encountered before were about vocabulary. Oh, you do need to master rhythms and rates, but if you know the basic words, you can participate in the discussion.

This isn't the process in Chinese. If all you had to do is master the words, life wouldn't be too tough because there aren't that many words. The problem is that one word has four meanings depending on whether your voice is going up or down or around while you are pronouncing it.

In other words, Chinese is a language of tones or voice inflections. These include rising, falling, straight, or down and up. Let me illustrate.

"Ma" with a straight tone means mother. "Ma" with a rising tone means flax. "Ma" with a falling tone means criticism. "Ma" with a down (falling) and up (rising) tone means horse. Are you ready for the test? Be careful how you say it lest you call my mother a horse.

Because of this tonal quality of the language, listening to a Chinese discussion is fascinating. It often sounds as if two people are singing to each other. Trying to speak it, on the other hand, is a challenge, particularly for someone as tone deaf as I am. Although I knew some of the vocabulary, I still never managed to make anyone understand what I was trying to say.

After complete frustration, I decided to keep silent and listen, thinking I might pick up some sense of the tones. That's when I learned another lesson about the Chinese language. It is full of expressions which I call vocalized trash.

We have these in English. As we participate in a discussion with a friend, we frequently punctuate our thoughts with utterances such as "Yeah," "Sure," "No," "Well, I'll declare," "Land of Goshen," "You don't say?" "Get out of here." Vocalized trash – expressions inserted for emphasis which don't really carry much meaning.

I suspect the Chinese may use more of these than even we do. For awhile, I thought they were trying to say something to each other with all those grunts and growls until I realized that this was verbal trash, but even that was spoken with proper inflections.

I would explain all this to you in Chinese, but I don't want to criticize your mother or your horse.

Nine Dragons

Son of the dragon; daughter of the phoenix. These symbols of China are steeped in thousands of years of tradition.

Unlike the Western dragon snorting fire and wreaking havoc, the Chinese dragon brings happiness, peace, and goodwill. In ancient China, the golden dragon was the symbol of the emperor while the phoenix was the symbol of the queen.

The Chinese dragon does not snort fire like his Western cousin. Instead he is the god of the waters in charge of rain, rivers, and even wells. In the Chinese legends, if the dragon ever did take human form, he turned into a beautiful and noble lady.

These legends are a significant part of the culture and can be traced all the way back to the earliest times. According to the stories, the nine parts of ancient China grew out of nine different dragons. That is why the nine-dragon theme is so prevalent in Chinese art, both in the past and even in the present. You see them everywhere, and Chinese of all ages find joy in telling you that they are descendants of the dragons.

One of the big holidays is Dragon Day which features the dragon dance. Several people will cooperate in putting on the dragon costume and marching and dancing through the streets amidst a display of fireworks. If they come to your house, you are destined to experience good fortune for the year.

The year 2000 was particularly pertinent because it was the Year of the Dragon – the year of tradition, of hope, of prosperity, and good fortune. Any child born in the Year of the Dragon will surely be special. In fact, some of our young married friends purposely waited until the year 2000 to have their baby because they wanted the best for their child.

Silly legends of antiquity? Superstitions from ancient times? Perhaps, but the nine dragon symbol still holds special meaning for Chinese people of all ages.

Black July

To say that the Chinese educational system is exam-driven is an understatement. The ubiquitous exam permeates all nooks and crannies – the textbooks, the curriculum, the classroom methods and the teachers' activities.

The students' minds are never more than seconds away from the inevitable exam, whether it's coming tomorrow or next week or at the end of the year or off in the long term future called Black July.

The exam is not the result of education. It is not a necessary requirement for measurement of learning. It is not the culminating achievement. It is much more than that. The exam is the purpose – for everybody, teachers and students alike, and this fact builds intensity the older a child gets.

To say that Chinese education is intense is an understatement. It is intense from Day One until Black July.

Children begin school at age six. Although exact numbers are difficult to obtain, I would guess that about ninety percent of the children do begin school. I have no idea what happens to the other ten percent, but the ninety percent who do go to school work at it. School days are long – six days a week – about 250 days a year. One of the major concerns across the country is the weight of their book bags. Some government representatives are appalled that the children have to carry such heavy bags, but parents and teachers protest that all the materials are necessary to prepare the children for the exams.

After six years of this kind of intensity, the children take the first major hurdle exam. About forty percent fail. The other sixty percent go on to junior high, or as they call it, junior middle school. Again the study is intense, all for one reason – to pass the exam which comes at the end of ninth grade. About forty percent fail. The rest go on. During high school, or senior high middle school, the intensity builds for the next three years. Six days a week the students study their lessons. On Sunday morning they take practice exams. They study vigorously, compete ferociously, and wallow in anxiety. There aren't any frills in the curriculum – no music, no art, and minimum physical education. These would all distract from the focus of preparing for the exams.

28

Even during vacations, there isn't much time for relaxing. Passing the exam is important to students and their teachers, but it is also important to parents. To say that the children's exam is important to parents is an understatement. This is the meaning of their lives – the principal reason for existence – the source of personal esteem. A student's failure would bring shame on the whole family. Thus, the family helps in the process by giving the student additional homework assignments to keep him focused during vacations.

After living through all this, the student finishes senior middle school about the first of July and soon plunges into three days of "The Exam" – the culminating moment of his education – of his whole life, actually. Based on their scores, the students are given their higher education options – admission to elite universities, comprehensive universities, normal schools for careers as teachers, business or technical specialized schools.

Those who make high marks win fame, honor, and joy for themselves and their families. Those who make low marks find shame and a sense of failure that paints the backdrop for a Black July!

This is how the exam-driven system works. What are the results? The most obvious is that the universities aren't bursting at the seams. The system does control enrollment with only about five percent of young people eventually getting to college. This is an important function in a highly populated, labor intensive society. Another result is that students are focused. The national exam produces a national curriculum, national textbooks, almost uniform teaching methods and a national purpose. In other words, the central government controls education all the way from the size of first graders' book bags to which facts the seniors memorize and which answers are the correct ones.

But at what cost? One hundred and twenty-five college sophomores and not one could play a musical instrument – had ever sung in a choir, had ever played in an organized sports event.

29

They had lived with twelve years of the threat of Black July which didn't give much time for the "frills" of education.

Three Gorges

By now every person in the world knows that one of the most scenic spots in China (and the whole world) is the Three Gorges area.

31

By now every person in the world knows that the Chinese are building a dam across the Three Gorges.

Is that dam necessary to supply basic needs? What are the Chinese trying to prove?

I don't know all the answers, but my friend Mr. Gu gave me a perspective to help understand it. After he had returned from a trip to Europe, he gave a report to my students about his experiences. One of his major impressions was sitting on a park bench in Paris and having the birds eat from his hand. As usual for Mr. Gu, he put it in philosophical terms. "The West," he told the students, "is a contractual society. They live in a contract relationship with their government, with each other, and with nature. We Chinese, on the other hand, don't have such a contract."

That little explanation helped me make meaning of what I saw. Rather than trying to find symbiosis, the Chinese seemed to be at war with nature. If they don't like where the mountain is, they move the mountain. If they don't like how the river flows, they change the river. If they don't want to cut the grass, they get rid of the grass.

One explanation for this is simply the Chinese sense of practicality. The richness of life is food and not natural beauty. They do what they have to do to make sure they have enough food to feed the population. But there seems to be another dimension of their actions lurking just beneath the surface of practicality. At times, it seems as if they tackle a project of changing nature just to prove that they can do it. I am not sure to whom they are proving it – to the rest of the world, to themselves or to nature herself.

In the summer of 1998, China was devastated by floods. The loss of life and property was sobering, sad, and enormous. But looming over this devastation was a deeper thought – the loss of security. For years, the Chinese have been cutting their forests and ignoring the problems of erosion. They were confident that they were winning the war against nature. But nature struck back in the form of record-setting rains, and they found themselves vulnerable. This was the lesson of the floods.

Now the government is actively involved in the Three Gorges Project. What they accomplish is a lesson for history to decide, but many of the people on the street are apprehensive, now that they have seen the force of nature through the floods.

Driving Rules

I am sure the Chinese have traffic laws. I even saw scenes of motorists stopped by the police for some infraction. But as a passenger riding along the streets, side roads, and super highways, I never could determine what those laws might be.

Fortunately for us Americans with our habits, the Chinese drive on the right side of the road. At least they are supposed to drive on the right side of the road. There are even dividing lines, but apparently, those are just suggestions to show where the middle is. They drive all over the road. One reason is that the road is filled with a variety of vehicles and obstacles all moving at a different rate of speed. This is true on city streets and on the super highways alike. In going from one city to another, the drivers stop, pay a toll and get on a nice concrete super-highway which is packed with cars going sixty miles per hour, trucks going fifty miles an hour, tractors pulling loads at thirty miles an hour, pedestrians going two miles an hour, and piles of drying rice not moving at all. It's not a drive down the interstate. It's an obstacle course.

I can't tell you whether these are four lane roads, six lane roads or eight lane roads, because the lines don't mean much. Vehicles may be four or five abreast in some spots, and if one side of the road is too crowded with obstacles, the drivers just pull over to the other side and hope that they win the chicken game against on-coming traffic.

In the heart of the city there is a little more order, but not much. As best as I could tell, there is no such concept as an illegal turn. The rule seems to be that you turn whenever it's convenient.

One of the features of downtown which did help is that traffic lights come equipped with clocks which show how much time is left on the red or green light. This does contribute to some order.

On the other hand, I was able to discern one very specific driving custom, if not law. The drivers are to use their horns more than their brakes. Regardless of what is in front of you, maintain speed and honk at it. If it can move, you're safe.

We did see accidents. Almost every time we left home, we saw some kind of an accident, usually just fender-benders and nothing serious. The surprising factor was that we didn't see more accidents, and the pleasant surprise is that we weren't in an accident!

The automobile business is booming all over China. Thousands of new drivers take to the road every month. I shudder to think of the consequences.

Peeled Grapes

The Chinese fertilize with human waste. Enough about that, except that this particular reality produces a strong set of rules.

Don't drink the water until you have boiled it for at least twenty minutes. This is a mandate not just for tourists and foreigners, but it is also obeyed by the Chinese themselves. Consequently, in recent years, the bottled water industry has grown in enormous leaps. Carrying a bottle of water to class or to the cinema or even while walking in the street is almost a fashion statement. It is what the chic people do.

Wash vegetables thoroughly and cook them well before eating.

Peel the fruit.

Of course, that is an easy rule to follow when you live among orange groves. In fact, we learned a new skill of putting our thumbs into the base of the orange, popping it open, and eating the slices right out of the peel.

The rule becomes a bit more difficult to implement when eating apples and pears, but we managed to be dutiful in peeling them first.

The problem for me was the grapes. I have just never been very skillful at peeling grapes. The grapes in our area of China are huge, plump and so inviting. When we visited in homes, they would always bring out the bowl of fruit to entice us, and there would be those grapes – purple and big enough to make your mouth water like you were a Pavlov dog.

So inviting that you couldn't resist until just as you picked it out of the bowl, the hostess handed you the peeling knife. For me, that was automatic mess time. I never mastered the art of peeling grapes gracefully.

The Fishhead Seat

The idea of a seat of honor at the table is not so unusual. Most families in America have some kind of official or unofficial seating scheme which features Papa's chair as a place of distinction.

Thus, it was easy for me to accept the concept at the official dinners and banquets in China. The honor seat reserved for the highest-ranking person present is the one with the back to the wall facing the door. That's the honor seat – obvious and logical; but who gets to sit there is not so obvious and logical. The honor is the subject of ceremonial debate – at every meal. There were times when I thought the issue was settled as soon as we walked into the room. When I was invited to break bread with the president of the university or the mayor of the city, it seemed obvious to me who should get the honor seat; but the ceremonial debate was still required. Regardless of how important the Chinese official might have been, his sense of graciousness and self-effacement would cause him to point, gesture, protest, and insist that I was more honored than he. My sense of shock, cultural disorientation and embarrassment caused me to protest back. Sometimes I won. Sometimes I lost.

As I became more experienced and the banquets became more elaborate, I became more sincere in my protest. In the process of the year, I learned a big lesson. Honor has its price.

Once you get into that seat everyone recognizes you as the most important person, including the servers. Once in the seat of honor, you get to eat the delicacies. The servers work particularly hard at making sure you eat the delicacies. While the rest of the crowd is having fried snake, you get to sip the blood. While the rest of the crowd is having boiled eggs, you get to eat the one hundred year old eggs (eggs that have been buried for thirty days). While the rest of the crowd gets to eat the fish, you get to eat the fish head with the eyeballs staring right at you.

As I learned, honor has its price!

Spring Festival

Think of your emotions of Christmas. Double that. Now you have some concept of the meaning of Chinese New Year which is also known as Spring Festival. To say that this is the biggest holiday of the year is to be guilty of making a gross understatement. This is the BIGGEST holiday of the year looming way above all others.

Because the date of the event is based on the lunar calendar much as our Easter, it comes on a different day every year, but almost always it comes in February.

The rituals of celebration are numerous, varied, and solidified by thousands of years of tradition. Probably the first rite of celebration is family togetherness. This is an important piece of information should you ever be anywhere in the Orient at this time of year. The Chinese want to be home for Spring Festival, and they will get home any way they can — planes, buses, trains, bicycles, or ox carts. Every piece of public transportation is crammed — beyond standing room only, and the roads are crammed as well. They're going home for the holidays.

School pupils and university students get off three or four weeks. Factories and businesses are closed. Building comes to a standstill, and the Chinese spend Spring Festival with their families. Keep in mind that this is the extended family and not just the nuclear version. We're talking about big groups and much travel to get there.

The celebration itself takes place on New Year's Eve with days of preparation. As is typical in most celebrations, food is the focal point. The New Year's dinner is special. The food choices vary in different parts of the country, but in our province the principal ingredients were fish and pork cooked in various shapes and styles. The chief objective of the meal is gluttony. Eat as much as you can.

After the meal, the dedicated Chinese stay up through the night to watch the coming dawn. They are aided in their state of being awake by the sounds and sights of exploding fireworks throughout the night. Now that technology has come to China, the urge to sing traditional songs and play traditional games has surrendered to the custom of watching the big celebration in Beijing on TV.

Although different families give different kinds of gifts, the principal gift is money packaged in a red envelope. When the children are young, parents present these gifts of money to their offspring. When the children grow up and get jobs of their own, the process is reversed and the children do the presenting of the money.

The next day, the first day of the New Year, people pile brightly wrapped gifts into a bag and travel from house to house visiting friends and relatives and leaving them good wishes and a small gift.

This is Chinese New Year, Spring Festival. If you want to understand how big it really is, ask a Chinese person you meet about it. Watch the eyes light up when he or she provides a description full of details and childhood memories.

The National Bird--The Building Crane

Someone told me that one out of every six building cranes at work all over the world is working in Shanghai. I don't know whether that is true or not, but the point is significant. China is building.

Everywhere China is building – in the big cities, the smaller cities, the towns, and even in the countryside. Some buildings are for much needed housing; some buildings are for offices and retail shops; and some buildings are for factories. Many of the buildings are large, and many go straight up. That's why building cranes are the most popular birds in the nation.

Not only are the Chinese building, but they are building rapidly. In August of 1998, crews came to the rice field adjacent to the university and drove in stakes representing instructions for some kind of development.

In March of 1999, we went to the spot to attend a ceremony for opening an eight-lane highway complete with four- to six-floor buildings flanking the road on both sides. I would call that a lot of building for eight months.

This activity provokes two different and conflicting emotions in me. First there is the sheer excitement in the vibrance, the dynamic, the bursting progress. These are truly exciting times in

China. China is catching up, moving ahead, making rapid progress in building its infrastructure, reflecting economic strength and national optimism.

But at the same time what is the price of all this progress? When crews build eight-lane highways across the rice field, where do the farmers now go to grow the rice?

In the process of moving ahead, what are they leaving behind?

It is always important to move forward, but which way is forward?

42

Tai Gui Le

I gave two writing assignments. I had the students write a letter to a friend trying to sell them their dictionary. I then had them write a note for the bulletin board stating that they had lost their new dictionary.

When I checked the letters for language, details, and organization, I found that 125 students had left out a critical piece of information on the first assignment. They forgot to state the expected price. On the second assignment, 125 students dutifully listed the price they had paid for the lost book. So I wrote 125 times two notes to the students suggesting these corrections.

That night, somewhere in between pleasant dreams and convicted conscious, I awoke with a sudden start and realized that for 250 times I had forgotten the concept of "tai gui le."

It is the basic idea of Chinese shopping. Simply translated, it means "too much."

In application, it generates the rules of the buying experience. Rule One: Never pay the posted price. Negotiate, negotiate, negotiate! Rule Two: Once you have bought it, boast to everybody about what you paid for it. Getting a bargain is a cherished virtue!

Chinese shoppers bargain everywhere. They bargain with the vendors on the street. They bargain in the small Mom and Pop shops. They even bargain in the department stores. It is all part of the experience. Parents teach the art form to their children, and being a good shopper is a noble character trait. Although attitude is important, timing seems to be the critical factor. You have to know when to look interested and when to walk away.

Once we stopped in a department store to check prices of purses. Mary was looking for a particular model, and not finding it, we left the store. One of the sales ladies came scurrying up the street to catch us and assure us that the prices posted on the purses were negotiable. The price is important, but for the Chinese merchants, the sale is the guiding force.

Now stir that information into the hopper, and let's see if we can make sense of the Chinese economic principles and theories.

This isn't capitalism. I know that because I made the mistake of calling it capitalism in the presence of some civic leaders. They told me in no uncertain terms that it is not capitalism. Capitalism, whatever it is, is bad. They know that because they read about it in Marx and in Chairman Mao and in the newspapers and magazines. Capitalism is the sin of the West – the tool of corruption and evilness and oppression. How dare we think that what they do is capitalism!

No, their system is socialistic market economy. I don't know what that means except that you had better learn to say "tai gui le" before you go on the shopping spree. Not only is your bankroll at stake, but your very personhood depends on your bargaining skills.

Praising Jessica

"I really enjoyed reading your essay. You know how to use the story to document your point. You are a very talented writer." I offered my sincere evaluation one day after class.

On hearing my words, Jessica bowed her head, studied her shoes, readjusted her book bag, and stood awkwardly avoiding any eye contact. She spoke just above a whisper, "I suppose my writing is sometimes not bad."

What was going on here? Had I broken some rule? Was I guilty of a cultural faux pas?

As an educator with forty years experience, I found Jessica's response to my evaluation to be one of the most difficult adjustments I had to make.

We had been warned about the Chinese cultural principle of self-effacement. I don't know who teaches them or what methods are used, but they learn the lesson well. They have a tough time accepting praise – anytime, anyplace, and from anybody.

We had been told to expect this from adults. "Mr. Wu, your wife is very pretty."

"Oh, no, she is common looking."

"Mrs. Wang, your son is a good student."

"He needs to study even harder. He is sometimes lazy." But I wasn't ready for it in the classroom.

Praise has always been one of my teaching tools. I don't use it indiscriminately, and I don't exaggerate, but I have always felt that students need to be told when they have accomplished something.

"Joe, I like your shirt."

"Margaret, your writing gets better every week."

"Sam, that's a great answer. How did you get so much wisdom at such an early age?"

As a product of my culture, I can use such statements easily – without hesitation and with sincerity.

As a product of their culture, the students responded awkwardly. They just weren't used to hearing such an appraisal of themselves. In fact, some students expressed dissatisfaction because I did not always write harsh, stern criticisms on their papers. They were expecting me to tell them the worst instead of the best.

Cultural faux pas or not, I am too old to change my methods, so I ignored their dissatisfaction and continued with my honest evaluations. Which reminds me! I need to send Jessica an e-mail today. She just sent me a copy of a short story she has written, and she wants my opinion. I must tell her truthfully. I like it!

Snakes, Snails, Eels and Turtles

Water is a prominent feature of the Chinese landscape. Although we have not been to all parts of the country, in the places where we have traveled, we have been impressed with the collection of water in such things as rivers, canals, lakes, and ponds ranging from two or three acres to holes in the ground.

In the places we have been, the weather has cooperated with ample amounts of rain. Last year in Jinhua, it rained every-day in April, and sometimes it rained all day.

Water is also part of the man-made beauty of the place. Last year, our university took on a major project of building a three-acre lake right in the middle of campus. Now that it is finished and full of water, it is beautiful, and it brings a lot of joy to our students and faculty alike.

Of course, the Chinese need water to produce their number one crop of rice. They flood their fields before planting, and they keep their fields flooded during most of the growing season. All this requires a large quantity of water.

The Chinese, always practical, not only eat the rice, but they also eat the other things that grow in the water, such as the fish, the snakes, the snails, the eels, and the turtles. These water creatures are almost as much a part of the daily diet as the rice itself.

We never managed to find any of these delicacies frozen or processed. The Chinese like to eat them fresh. Thus, as you walk through the front door of the restaurant, you pass by tanks and tanks of water creatures swimming around. One of the duties of the customer is to choose the particular species which the chef is to prepare for supper. It adds one more interesting dimension to the process of elegant dining. But the result is worth learning the custom. There is nothing more delicious than turtle soup prepared by a Chinese chef just for your unique palate.

48

Momma

The first word each of our three children learned to say was "Momma," and we will never forget the moment – the excitement, the pride, the thought that they were beginning to master their own language by identifying a relationship with the person they love.

Imagine our surprise when we discovered that the first word the Chinese children learn to say is "Momma." Isn't that amazing?

Since mastering "Momma," our children have learned a few other words, too, and we know every one of those words. The Chinese children have learned a few other words, too, but we don't know one of those. But it is still amazing that children in both countries started language at the same place.

Although we haven't traveled all over the world and encountered every known language, we do know that this is the same in Russia. They, too, start with "Momma," and then move into the rest of the language. We give you this information and let you draw your own conclusions.

What does it mean? Universals? Absolutes? Universals in language? Absolutes in human emotion?

You are on your own to decipher this. But I just get excited to think that regardless of where I am, every person I see on the street probably said "Momma" as his or her first word. It just makes us all seem a little closer together, doesn't it?

The Sixth Floor

I have always been fascinated to discover how some cultures attach peculiar attributes to specific numbers, such as lucky seven or unlucky thirteen. Although I don't understand all the implications, the Chinese apparently put great significance on the number six because that is how many floors the buildings have.

This is particularly true with residential buildings. All over the country in all different kinds of work units, people live in six story buildings. Just recently, our friend Chen invested his money in erecting an apartment building for non-traditional students who have to provide their own living accommodations. How large is the building? Six floors, of course. Maybe they build six floors for some practical reason such as saving architect fees.

Although all the buildings look very much alike and each floor is almost identical, there is still some kind of pecking order attached to the assignment of residence on each specific floor. The first floor is the least desirable because it's too close to the noise and trash of the outside. The choice floor, logically enough, is the third floor – high enough to avoid the disturbances of an outside world but still not all the way to the top.

Well, that's what they tell us. We can't attest to it personally. All our friends, colleagues, and remotest acquaintances live on sixth floor. That's right! Sixth floor – all the way to the top with no elevator anywhere to be found! We have no firsthand proof that any living person resides on the first five floors.

We heard "Sixth floor" so often that we got to the point that we could anticipate it.

"Could you come to our house for supper?"

"Oh, we would love to. Where do you live?"

"Building 27 – middle gate – sixth floor. You can't miss us."

Sixth floor. I don't know what is worse – going up, climbing flight by flight, wearing out your knees and getting light headed as the air gets thinner, and arriving at the door too out of breath to ring the bell, or having to come down after spending a pleasant evening of frivolity having laughed yourself silly and eaten way too much of the most delicious Chinese food you have ever tasted!

The good news is that the pain of going up and coming down is the kind that you don't remember too long so that you are ready the next time someone asks, "Could you come for supper? Building 27, middle gate, sixth floor."

Rice on the Road

With more than a billion people, China's number one priority is food production. Even with all the high rise construction, the growing economy, and the burgeoning technology, food production still takes precedence over all other enterprises.

The motivating factor is memory. The middle-aged generation can still recall times when, as children, they had meals of fried grass and Papa got one bowl of rice a day to give himself enough energy to do his job. Although food is in good supply now, the times of near starvation are close enough in their history that they still appreciate the luxury of abundance.

Even with all the business people, merchants, educators and builders, most Chinese people are still farmers actively involved in food production. Rather than establishing the huge collective farms as in the communistic Soviet Union, the Chinese government distributed the land in small plots of about six acres to individual families. Although a few of the really rich families have a water buffalo to pull the plow, most of the work is done by hand — literally by hand! They work from morning until night in all kinds of weather — sun and rain. Although there is a wide variety of crops, the staple is rice on almost every farm, and the farmers produce one, two, or three crops a year depending on the climate in that particular area.

Watching the process as I traveled along the roads, I have concluded that rice production requires a great deal of hard work.

Just preparing the field for planting, farmers slosh around in six inches of water and fertilizer made from human waste. They then put the seedlings in place plant by plant. During the growing season, they are always walking through their fields searching for weeds which they stomp into the ground with their foot rather than chopping with a hoe.

All that work is only the precursor to harvest time. They cut the rice with a scythe, tie it into bundles, and carefully put it into stacks. When the stalks are dry and the grain is ripe, they run the bundles through a hand propelled threshing machine which beats the grain out of the head.

When they get that far, they are only half finished. They now must spread it over a flat dry surface, and turn it and beat it for several days as they eliminate the husks and other waste materials.

But here is the problem. What do they use for that flat dry surface? The answer: with food production as the top priority in the nation, farmers use anything they can find for spreading their rice, and any other activities scheduled for that space will just have to wait for the rice to dry.

The favorite spot for drying rice is the road – big roads, small roads, concrete bridges, or super highways – it doesn't matter. In China, producing food is more important than the convenience of getting somewhere.

If you ever spend some time defining accomplishment of purpose, ponder this: more than one billion people in China, and I saw an abundance of food.

Xu, Wu, and Everyone Else

In all cultures, the study of names offers us valuable data in understanding historical movements and social constructs. I'm sure there are lessons to be learned from the character of Chinese names; I just don't know what they are, but I do know some of the facts.

The first name that identifies a person is actually the family name, or more specifically, the father's family name. When a woman marries, she keeps that family name; it is hers permanently. The second name is the one chosen by the parents to distinguish this particular child, and these names often have some meaning such as a season of the year, a personality trait, or a favorite flower.

From surveying our students' names, we made a couple of observations. For one thing, certain names are quite common. The Smith, Jones, and Johnson names of China appear to be Xu, Wu, and Chen. In one class of twenty-four, three students had the family name of Chen, and they vehemently rejected the idea that they might be related to one another.

Another interesting characteristic is in the writing of the name. All names, and all rosters, of course, are properly written in Chinese characters. Sometimes, such rosters as class rolls, will have the pinyin (Roman alphabet) along with the Chinese characters. This plays havoc with any attempt at alphabetical order. So the Chinese are accustomed to numerical arrangements rather than alphabetical.

Mary and I ran into one other small problem with the family name. Of course, they couldn't understand how we both had the same family name until we explained how it works in marriage in the United States – a novel idea for them. The big problem, however, came at the bank. The school officials suggested that it would be convenient for them and safer for us to receive our salary by direct deposit. We dutifully marched off to the bank for the simple process of opening an account. That's when we learned a big lesson about Chinese family names. They are short – two, three, or four letters, and on rare occasions, maybe as many as five, but no way is a handle as long as Schimmels going to get into a Chinese bank computer. Panic was calmed and peace was restored by a simple solution. At the bank, our accounts can be found under the identifying names of Clif with one "f" and Mary – only four letters each.

Strolls

Some cultural customs should be turned into international law. One such nomination would be the Chinese ritual of the after-supper stroll. In all seasons and in all kinds of weather, it is a regularly scheduled daily activity for many people.

This isn't a walk. It isn't a hike or a jog designed to score aerobic points. It is a stroll – a casual, slow-paced, non-directional stroll.

Some strolls are family-oriented – father, mother and child out together – walking, talking, playing, examining the universe.

Some strolls are friendship-oriented – good friends get together to chat, bond and stroll without interruptions and time constraints.

Some strolls are personal-oriented – an opportunity to get out by yourself away from the activities of the day to reflect, plan, or dream, all under the routine of a stroll.

You don't need me to point out the therapeutic value of these strolls. It's obvious. The blood pressure, the digestive system, the cardio-vascular system, the joints and muscles, friendships and families are all benefactors.

Wouldn't it be wonderful to weave such an activity into American culture? Could we even compute the gains to emotional and physical health of the society?

But that's a far away dream. I just don't expect any immediate miracles in that direction.

Even something as seemingly simple as the after-supper stroll is a Chinese art form handed down through several generations. Although we Americans might be able to imitate the mechanics of the stroll, I think we are still years away from grasping the spirit of it.

English Corner

What do our students do on Sunday afternoons? They take a couple of hours off to relax by spending some time at a low-pressure event called English Corner. This is not just an activity on our campus, but it is something of a nationwide institution.

You find them on university campuses, in parks of the big cities, and at the People's Squares in towns and villages.

Very simply, the English learners in the community come together to practice their oral communication skills.

In some places, such as on our campus, there are planned activities. Students work hard during the week putting together a program of songs, poems, riddles, skits, games, debates, and free talk — something for everyone.

In other places, the English speakers just meet together to talk.

The rules are simple. Anyone is welcome, and participants come from all ages and all walks of life. The only other rule is English only. For a couple of hours a week, the Chinese come together to practice a foreign language.

No one takes attendance. There are no exams. There is no accountability. People come because they want to.

There is a message to us in the whole concept of the English Corner – maybe many messages.

Just to think that so many Chinese people are that interested in practicing English that they will give up a couple of hours on a Sunday afternoon is almost overwhelming. What does it show? Love of the language? Desire to learn? A need to socialize?

Whatever the reason for the success of English Corner, the obvious reality is that across the nation, millions of Chinese are very interested in learning our language and learning as much about us as they can.

I once heard that there are more students of English in China than in America. I don't know whether that's true, but I am confident of one fact. There are more Chinese learning English than there are Americans learning Chinese.

Two Caucasians and an African

Pauline came from Cameroon to spend two years learning the language so she can go back to her country to start a Chinese department in the university. That's just one example of how China is establishing political, economic and cultural exchanges with various nations around the world.

Pauline is a neat lady – a dedicated student, a committed teacher, a devout Christian, and a good friend. We worked together frequently. We spoke at schools together. We shopped together. We dined together. We created spectacles together.

In our city, many miles away from the urban and tourist centers of the country, people going about their daily routines don't expect to see foreigners on the street or in the buses, so the sight of two rather large Caucasians was enough to bring stares and sometimes even interruptions of activity.

Add to that attraction a black woman, and you have a formula for chaos. To put it mildly, the average Chinese people just don't expect to see black people walking around their city.

Early in the year, Mary and I and Pauline accompanied our friend, Issa, into the city one Saturday evening. Our plan was to have a leisurely supper in a restaurant and spend the evening strolling around the streets, the shops and the river.

We had no intentions of creating havoc, but we did. Everywhere we went, people stared. People walking along the streets stopped and stared, creating pedestrian jams. People racing by on bicycles turned to stare and crashed their bicycles into objects and each other. Even taxi drivers stared, endangering themselves and their passengers.

We became frightened – not for ourselves, but for everyone else in the downtown area that evening, so we caught the nearest taxi and went home before we created the next day's headlines – "Four People Killed in Bicycle Wrecks Caused by the Spectacle of Two Caucasians and an African!"

Layers

"There is no heat south of the river," my friend Murl once told me. In other words, the Yangtze River cuts a swath across the nation that just about divides China into a north and a south; and Murl, who had lived and traveled in China in the 1980's, was telling me something basic that someone should know. I remembered what he said. I filed the information away somewhere in the back of my subconscious unaware that that one simple statement would become so paramount to my basic survival.

In October, I realized the full meaning of a simple sentence. There is no heat south of the river. We were in Jinhua in Zhejiang Province, about 300 miles south of the river. As soon as we arrived in August, we ascertained that the climate would be about like what we were accustomed to in our native Tennessee – hot in the summer, rather warm in the fall and spring, and mild winters with some freezing and snow mixed in for a few days at a time. We were correct in that analysis. But we forgot to remember that there is no heat south of the river. We forgot until October. That's when we woke up one crisp autumn morning with a nip in the breeze and frost on the pumpkin. There is no heat south of the river. There was no heat in the bedroom, no heat in the living room, no heat in the bathroom, no heat in the classrooms, no heat in the restaurants, no heat in the homes of our friends – no heat anywhere. No heat on a crispy morning in October, and no heat during the three-day snow storm in January. To be emphatic, there is no heat south of the river. Do you know what it is like to go to one of the most expensive restaurants in town and sit there watching your breath blow out of your mouth? So how do you cope with no heat? Two methods – layers and ingenuity. In Jinhua, people dressed in layers. Because I did not watch them put the layers on or take them off, I really don't have an accurate account of how many layers they wear or what they are, but they wear layers – at least four or five. Having lived in Chicago for awhile, I had known something about the virtues of layers because you could remove some should the temperature rise, but for the Chinese, there wasn't much removing. They just wore all the layers all the time – in other words, full coats in the house. In fact, to make sure the layers were necessary, they would open windows in classrooms before the body temperature could change the climate much. I later learned the practical reason for that. Body heat in a cold damp room creates a serious humidity problem, and they opened the windows to keep from sticking to the papers they were writing.

Of course, as cold as it was, the students wore gloves. They wore gloves to class, and they wore gloves during class. To be able to take notes clearly, they wore gloves with removable fingers. What a neat invention – a full pair of woolen gloves with the forefinger and thumb removed to allow for the flexibility of taking a clear set of notes!

Another trick they developed was to carry a jar of hot green tea all day long. This was not necessarily for sipping, but for wrapping their hands around.

In the spirit of being south of the river, Mary and I donned our layers and joined the activities of winter. Our problem was that we had one set of layers for daytime and another set to wear to bed, and the excruciating moment of the day was transition. For awhile, we turned it into a race. We tried to discover how quickly we could get out of one set of five layers into another set of five layers with all the motion taking place in a room several degrees below freezing. As it got even colder, we lost the race, and realized that we would have to become ingenious, or we would freeze some night before we could get in bed.

At that point, we discovered the appeal of the American movie. We had brought many films, more than we could ever show to the large groups, so we started showing films to our classes at night in our living room. A class of twenty-five jammed in, sitting shoulder to shoulder for two hours, either warmed by mild hilarity of the scenes or by the love story, whichever was available, brought enough heat into our home that we managed the nightly ritual of dressing for bed, even south of the river, where there is no heat.

65

Chinese Backhoe

Labor Intensive Country! Labor Intensive Country! Labor Intensive Country! The slogans flap around in the wind until they beat the life out of themselves and turn into cliches. What does it mean – labor intensive country? The slogan is sterile enough, but the reality in practice is still almost awesome – every time!

In March, we got new telephone cables all across campus, and the workers came to bury the lines – dig the ditches, cut through the streets and sidewalks, install the new lines and replace all disruptions. The work went fast. The whole project took less than two weeks, and the most sophisticated machine used was a wheelbarrow. All that work accomplished with picks, shovels, and labor. It was a sight to behold. Two hundred men and women arriving early and staying late, working almost in unison on a common project which they may or may not understand.

My questions come in quantity. Who are these people? How did they choose or get chosen for this line of work? How much do they get paid? When are their holidays?

Whom do they work for? A union? A contractor? Are they individuals waiting around for an opportunity such as this?

I didn't learn much about these people for a couple of reasons. For one thing, they weren't around too long – just came, did the job, and left. But the people from my world – university students and professors - never interacted with them, never even established eye contact. Although at times they were as close as three feet, they lived in two different worlds. The distance between them was almost eerie.

But the big question is what is the future of that human backhoe? It isn't a question of technology. China is already there. As a country, they have the equipment and tools to replace those people tomorrow. Maybe the equipment could do the work even tidier and more efficiently.

But what is to become of those people with the picks and shovels?

68

Green Tea

Beverage of choice? Panacea? Ceremonial drink? Green tea is all of the above, and the Chinese drink it morning, noon, and night.

To the uninitiated, green tea is just green tea; but to the expert, which is any Chinese person by matter of birth, green tea comes in varying degrees of quality and taste. There is this year's crop, last year's crop, the spring crop, the autumn crop, north tea, south tea. To distinguish between those differences is not something you can learn. You just have to be born into that knowledge.

The process of making green tea is no mystery. You just sprinkle a few leaves into a cup and pour in hot water – the hotter the better.

The trick is in drinking it – sipping that hot tea without getting your teeth full of leaves. That, too, must be a natural born talent because I know of no American who has ever mastered it.

The only other secret is to keep adding hot water every time the guest takes a sip. In Chinese culture, the poor host is one who lets the tea get cold. As a native born U.S. southerner, this strikes me as amusing. The Chinese, world-class experts on the subject, find the whole concept of iced tea to be unthinkable and repulsive.

Some drink their tea cup by cup. Some make tea in a jar early in the morning and carry it with them all day just adding hot water on occasions. Whatever the particular style, they drink their tea. It's more than a part of their diet. It's a part of their lifestyle.

They claim great therapeutic value in the beverage. It calms their nerves, helps them avoid weight gain, controls the heart-beat, aids in digestion, soothes sore throats, and clears the mind.

All this may or may not be true, but the real value of green tea is ceremonial. Chinese society and business revolves around the cup of tea.

The law of tradition requires that any visitor in any home anywhere must have a cup of hot tea in his hand from the moment he arrives to the moment he leaves. This applies to all circumstances. Even when we visited friends in hotel rooms, we were served the ceremonial cup of tea despite the hardship in finding the materials to make it.

At business meetings, the ceremony is built into the agenda. Regardless of the negotiations and transitions at hand, or the tensions that might arise, we start with a hot cup of tea and casual conversation.

All that ceremony may not meet the standards of efficiency, but we can't argue with the results considering how much worldwide business the Chinese are doing now. Perhaps there is some special power in the tea.

Bamboo

I can't imagine what China would be without bamboo, arguably the greatest crop on the planet. The Chinese use it for everything.

First, they eat it. Bamboo shoots prepared by Chinese cooks, who are artists in aprons anyway, are delicious. Apparently, these tasty plants are plentiful in certain parts of the country. An old adage describes anything of rapid growth as springing up like bamboo shoots.

Apparently, people are not the only ones to eat the bamboo. We are told that this is the staple diet of the pandas as well.

What's amazing is that something so delicious can grow up to become such a useful and durable product. A botanist tried to explain it to me, but I didn't understand. All I know is that bamboo is one of the toughest materials known to man with a multitude of uses.

By slicing it into two parts, the Chinese make a lightweight shoulder pole for carrying heavy loads balanced across the body. They use bamboo for building construction scaffolding, for building the beds of their bicycle pick-up trucks, for building sidewalks and door jams, for supporting roofs, for pry bars. If the job requires something tough, durable, but lightweight, there is a bamboo pole just right for the assignment.

As I said, what would China be without it?

Seventh Grade Dormitories

"Dr. Schimmels, I want to practice writing more. Could you give me a topic to write about which would let me practice my English and perhaps get something published?" Margaret is not only a gifted writer, but she is an eager learner.

"Sure, Margaret! Why don't you write a paper describing your parents – what they do, and how they relate to you. As good as you write, we may even get this published in an American magazine," I suggested.

"But you have always told us to write about what we know best," she protested.

"Of course, that's why you could write about your parents," I encouraged her.

"That's the problem." She dropped her voice. "I don't know my parents very well. I have been living in dormitories since I was in the seventh grade, and I only see my parents twice a year during holidays."

Sometimes it is refreshing to teach in a country where education is recognized as a privilege. Sometimes it is depressing to teach in a country where education is recognized as a privilege.

The Chinese know that education is a privilege – a life-changing privilege. With an education, you can teach, administrate, doctor, experiment or travel. Without an education, you can plant rice by hand, hammer big rocks into small ones or dig ditches. There is quite a difference in quality of life between the two.

Everyone knows that – children, parents, and teachers. Because they do know the privilege of an education, they are willing to make some sacrifices.

With the sheer volume of people who want to go to school, there just simply aren't enough schools. There aren't enough buildings. There aren't enough textbooks. There aren't enough teachers.

If the remote villages are able to manage a school at all, the best they can hope for is an elementary school through grade six. Those students who pass the exam and are invited to continue must then make the decision to leave their homes and parents and board at school.

74

Depending on their exam scores, the students are invited to study at specific schools which are ranked for their reputations of excellence. It's easy to tell which are which. The best-rated school is called Number One Middle School. The second best is called the Number Two Middle School, etc. The students make their choices on factors rather than proximity to their homes and parents; thus, we have seventh graders living in dorms who only see their parents twice a year, and we have university students who don't know their own parents well enough to write about them.

Before I spent a year in China, I had heard stories about the family structures, the richness of family life, the role of parents in shaping their children. Frankly, I was always a bit envious of what I thought they had, and then I met Margaret.

Queues and Non-Queues

Educators speak of the hidden curriculum – those lessons we package inside our methodology so skillfully that we inculcate a whole generation of children without their even knowing it. Often we are so good at the hidden curriculum that we don't even know we're teaching it.

Chief among those lessons in American society is the Nobility of the Line. We teach lines. Line up to go to the bathroom. Line up to get a drink. Line up to enter the room. Nice children stand quietly in lines. One of the seven major sins is to cut in line. In short, we teach, and teach effectively, that the line is noble!

One of the first and most lasting impressions for any Westerner in China is the fact that the queue is learned behavior. It is not a natural, instinctive lesson of the human race. In other words, the Chinese don't line up. They simply haven't learned that lesson.

We speak of mastering some basic survival skills as we prepare to enter another culture. Well, if you are planning to go to China, put this one at the top of the list. Chinese don't line up. They don't line up to go to the bathroom. They don't line up to get on the bus. They don't line up at the post office. They don't line up at the bank. They don't line up at the KFC counter.

According to the number one lesson of the American hidden curriculum, they break all the rules. They push, shove, crowd and cut in front of the less aggressive.

This was one of the most difficult adjustments we had to make during the entire year. Although we didn't realize it, the concept of line was so interwoven into our very personhood that we just couldn't adjust to the crowding. Not only that, we passed judgement on the Chinese – rude, arrogant, selfish people who crowd in front. How dare they break one of the principal rules of human decency?

Finally, we grew to the point that we could accept this difference in culture. We accepted their behavior, but we still couldn't do it. We just couldn't force ourselves to go against our creed, so when we went to the bank, or the post office, or KFC, we always took someone with us who had not learned to stand in the proper line to use the bathroom during their kindergarten year.

Chopsticks

I have a puzzle. Why is it that half the world eats with knives and forks while the other half uses chopsticks? What is the origin of this distinctive feature of culture? More importantly, what are the sociological and psychological implications of that marked difference between the East and the West? Can we ever fully understand each other with such a significant factor separating our worlds?

I exaggerate only slightly. I do think there is some kind of symbolic meaning in understanding the principles of eating with chopsticks. I just don't know what it is.

For the Chinese, the whole ritual of mealtime is based around the function of the chopsticks. Our friends, college educated middle class types, don't understand the American idea of lunch as a hamburger, French fries and coke. They seek a bit more variety. A usual lunch consists of four or five dishes that are all placed on the table at once. Individual diners have no individual place settings other than the chopsticks - a small saucer and a small bowl, if anything. With the chopsticks extending their arm spans by at least four inches, they reach to the dishes in the center of the table, get a mouthful in their grasp and proceed with the meal. They eat everything with the chopsticks except soup for which they have a spoon. There are no finger foods in China. Nothing is to be touched with the human hands. If you want a description of dexterity, try drawing a mental picture of a person eating a piece of fried chicken with chopsticks or even a biscuit filled with meat.

Actually, some foods make more sense eaten with chopsticks than with forks. One example is noodles. Of course, to use the chopsticks effectively, you have to employ a Chinese table manner law which says it's all right to slurp. Thus, you put the noodle in your mouth by using the sticks, and you take care of the rest of the process with a giant slurp. It may not sound too pretty, but it is still more attractive than the mess I make when I try to eat spaghetti with a fork.

Of course, there is a whole social commentary within the different kinds of chopsticks. This in itself is not unusual. Most of us have at least three categories of silverware ranging from plastic to the formal stuff that we receive as wedding gifts and only use at Christmas and Thanksgiving.

When you go out to eat with friends, you get a throwaway set of crude wooden sticks, just whittled out of a pine tree somewhere. When you go to the finer restaurants, you get the highly decorated sticks which impress you as part of the décor chosen specifically by someone with a sense of taste for balance and coordination.

In homes, families take pride in their different collections. Some families have even personalized their chopstick collection with details of color or textures or even construction.

As I watched my students and my friends eat with their chopsticks, I sat there amazed at how gently and casually they employed a skill so difficult and foreign for me, and as I went from home to home and restaurant to restaurant encountering the different types of chopsticks, I realized that there is something in their culture, in every culture in fact, which makes them unique and which the outsider can probably never fully comprehend.

Neck Bruises

When Shirley came to class with bruises on her neck, I was frightened. She is such a gentle lamb. Although her oral English is quite good, she spoke so softly in class that I had difficulty hearing. She was always the embodiment of Chinese feminine gentility – never loud, never boisterous, muffled laughter – gentle and charming. And she had a propensity to poetry. That was the thread in our relationship. She would fill her papers with quotations or original verses, and I would respond with similar genre. Although we didn't talk that much, we were close friends. At least, I thought so.

Then one day, Shirley came to class with ugly bruises all over her neck – red and puffy and threatening. It looked as if someone had tried to strangle her, and I, with my American public school training, was wondering which authority I should contact to report abuse. It was obvious that something was wrong.

The only other possibility would have been an over-zealous boyfriend; but I had never seen her with anyone, and she made no attempt to conceal the evidence.

There was something incongruous about those marks. I could have understood such bruises on an athlete or maybe even on one of the more flirty girls, but they were out of place on Shirley.

Fortunately, I didn't say anything. I had the urge. I wanted to investigate, to root out the culprit, and even take part in the punishment. But I didn't. I just kept quiet – partly because I was a foreigner and partly because no one else seemed to notice.

But the bruises haunted me – woke me up in the middle of the night. A couple of days later, with concern and curiosity blended together, I mustered the confidence to mention those marks to Mrs. Huang.

"Oh," she answered nonchalantly. "We do that all the time when we are not feeling well. We pinch our necks to get the blood flowing to our heads."

Whoops! Just another dimension of that great mystery called Chinese medicine.

During our year, we purposely stayed healthy so we could avoid first hand contact with doctors, hospitals, and Chinese medicine. Thus, all we know is what we picked up by eavesdropping and reading absence excuses.

Although there are hospitals, doctors, pharmacies, surgery and injections, in health care as in most of Chinese life, the old meets the new, and traditional medicine abounds. "It's all herbs," they would tell us. "No chemicals! No side effects." Then they would drink the prescribed potion by the quart.

Interestingly enough, the one form of treatment which we did not see and heard no reference to was acupuncture. Perhaps it was there, and we just didn't see it.

But we did see the neck bruises. After that initiation with Shirley, they became rather commonplace, particularly during flu season and during final exam times. I never asked anyone about the procedure, and no one discussed it. It is obviously a way of life.

I also never got up the courage to ask them if they could attest to the therapeutic value of pinching their own necks. Of course, I never got up the courage to tell them that my mother soaked my infections in kerosene and made me drink lemon juice and honey for my sore throats.

The Only Child

I taught college sophomores. Most of my students had brothers and sisters. Mary taught freshman. Most of her students did not have any brothers and sisters.

As we talked to those students, it was easy to pin point the exact year of the one-child policy. Regardless of what we might have heard in the United States, it is a reality. Families are now limited to one child.

There is one legal exception. In the farm homes, if the first child is a girl, they may have another in hopes of getting a boy to help with the work.

With the policy rigidly enforced, families work hard at birth control practices; but if they should miscalculate, and pregnancy occurs, they have no option but to abort. This, too, is a way of life.

I have no idea how long it will take for the one-child policy to make an impact on the size of the population, but it has produced some immediate points of interests.

With only one child, parents pour all their love, all their indulgence, and all their expectations on this one unfortunate person who has to work alone to carry out the family pride. Of course, children are not stupid, and they often respond by becoming active, independent, and possessive. In other words, they are spoiled. Some social scientists are calling these folks the Little Emperors.

Teachers have contributed with their evaluations. According to some educators, children without brothers and sisters have never learned how to share or cooperate or even play with others. Thus, the school has inherited the additional responsibility of helping students develop social skills.

Whether the one-child policy accomplishes its expected outcome in population control, it does provide a rich field for sociological study.

Colour, Flavour and Confuzion

The Chinese are learning English – en masse! In some places, children begin as early as kindergarten, but across the country, all students are required by law to study English from primary school through four years of university.

Simply stated, the Chinese are learning English. But which English are they learning? Sometimes we are wrapped up in our own worlds so tightly, that we forget that English comes in several different styles – an American style, a British style, an Australian style and even a Canadian style. In the midst of that comes the original and creative Chinese style of English – a combination of all of the above.

Just the differences between American and British English are enough to cause our heads to spin. There are differences in pronunciation – the broad "A" sound, for example, in words such as class, grass and plant.

There are differences in vocabulary. We say flashlight; they say torch. We say two weeks; they say fortnight. We say semester; they say term. We say student; they say pupil.

There are differences in spelling – color or colour, connection or connexion.

Now, try to see all this through the eyes of a Chinese student working to master the language of foreigners. His textbook was co-written by a British and a Chinese scholar and published in England. His supplementary tapes are from the recording labs in London. As an extra-credit assignment, he listens to a BBC broadcast.

Finally, he gets an opportunity to fulfill the dream of any serious foreign language student. He gets to meet a real live native speaker; and that person just happens to be American born, raised in Oklahoma cotton fields, influenced by seventeen years in Chicago, and now camped out in southeast Tennessee.

Can you even conceive of the confusion? What that poor student meets in real life is not even remotely close to what he learned from his book, tapes and teachers. Now what is he to think about English?

The students at our university were fortunate enough to have native English teachers three years in a row – one from Scotland, one from Australia, and one from Bradley County, Tennessee. Did I say that they were fortunate?

Spouses and Choices

"How did you two meet and fall in love?" the students asked when they came to the apartment. Regardless of the mission of the visit, the conversation would almost always come around to our marriage relationship.

We don't mind, though. We like telling the story, although it isn't all that dramatic. We met in freshman English class, dated some, drifted apart, came back together two years later, fell in love, got married, lived together for forty-two years, and we are still finding new dimensions of our relationship every day.

After we had heard the question over and over, and after we had told our story just as often, we arrived at an interesting insight. Sometimes we testify to the power of God in our lives intentionally and deliberately with planned speeches and discourses. But more often than that, we testify quietly, unintentionally, and accidentally just through the process of being.

Mary and I provided an intriguing study for the Chinese, both students and teachers alike. I don't know whether we are an unusual couple, but we are together. In almost everything we do, we are together. We are so together that people often refer to us with no-space between our names. We are known as CliffandMary. Beyond the fact that we like each other, there is a logical reason for the closeness. It has to do with strengths and weaknesses. What she does well, I don't, and what I do well, she doesn't. We need each other to make a complete team.

Our relationship was our most powerful witness during our year in China. The Chinese just didn't expect this from an American marriage. What they saw in us did not coincide with what they had read in the textbooks and had seen on television. They weren't ready for CliffandMary.

After they had time to adjust their thinking a bit and come to the realization that generalizations are not always accurate, they began to look at our relationship at even a deeper level – as something of a study of how marriage should work in any culture.

Until rather recently, love was not necessarily a factor in Chinese marriages. For our students' grandparents, and sometimes even their parents, marriage was a matter of convenience arranged by the families of the two young people who were destined to spend the rest of their lives together.

Because of these situations in their recent past, our students didn't have a really good operational definition of love. Of course, that is probably true of university students around the world. Most of them don't know what love is and have not always been wise in choosing appropriate models.

But it seemed to us that our Chinese students carried this emotion even further. It seemed as if they were a bit frightened about the awesome responsibility of choosing the right mate. They asked about our relationship, not because they were making polite conversation, but because they really wanted to know what kept us close for forty-two years after we had exchanged our vows.

As typical university students, they were interested in love stories. Their favorite American novel is *Gone with the Wind*. Although they admire the spunky heroine, they are captivated by the love story. While watching movies such as *Pretty Woman* and *While You Were Sleeping,* they sat with their eyes glued to the screen, and they cheered when love won out.

But as we studied their reactions, we came to believe that they were driven by something deeper than appreciation or fantasy. They were searching for a definition for love which they could apply to their lives as they practiced a rather newly-developed freedom of choosing a mate.

In the meantime, they studied CliffandMary intensely every moment they could. We can only pray that we silently said to them that we learned how to love each other because we know that Jesus loved us first.

87

A Quotation a Day

Several years ago, I developed the habit of putting a quotation for the day on the board for each class I teach. That is all it is – just a habit. I pick something I like – something pertinent to the lesson, something pertinent to the day, something pertinent to the way I am feeling – just anything, and I write it in one spot on the board. I rarely call attention to it, much less make a lesson from it. It is just an added thought on the board.

Through the years, I have had some interesting responses. Quite frequently, I will see some of the quotations come back to me on students' papers or in their speeches. Parents have told me that their children had told them the quotation. Some former students have even come back to tell me how much they remember the quotation on the board. Of course, those are the positive responses. Most of them, I must admit, aren't all that encouraging. In fact, I'm sure that most students don't even notice the quotation for the day. But I don't want to dwell on that possibility just now. As an old timer, I like to recall the positive more than the negative.

In China, last year, I kept up the activity. As I said, it's a habit, and I'm not very good at breaking habits. I would choose quotations from American or British literature or politics or

life in general and put them on the board, and just let them
speak for themselves. I wasn't sure what to expect from my
endeavor, but soon I noticed that some of the students were
using the quotations in their writing or in their oral presentations. In fact, some of the students were writing the quotations
down, taking them home and memorizing them on a daily
basis. To say the least, I found that response encouraging.

The amazing part of this whole activity was how often the
students would come into the class, look at the quotation for
the day, and exclaim, "Oh, that's great. We have a quotation just
like it in Chinese." Then they would give me their similar gem
of wisdom from Chinese culture, and we would compare the
meanings and backgrounds. This happened often – several times
a week, but the most surprising was that it happened when my
selection for the day was a quotation from the Bible.

In fact, I caught this reaction on the very first Bible quotation I used. Although I wasn't afraid of using the wisdom of the
Bible for a daily quotation, I had avoided the topic for a few
weeks because I still wasn't sure what the official reaction
would be. I was not afraid of any consequences for myself, but I
didn't want to trap my students in the middle should their
leader think that they were being taught the Bible in the foreigner's class. One day, the central focus of the lesson was
teacher merit pay, and it just seemed to me to be appropriate
to use the old admonition from Paul's letter to Timothy. "The
love of money is the root of all evil." With only a bit of trem-
bling, I wrote it on the board and waited for the students to
come in to register their surprise or complaints. When they
read it, they reacted in an outburst, "Oh, we have a quotation
just like that in Chinese," and they recited it for me.

Now I'm confused. I got the same reaction from every Bible
quotation I used. What's the meaning of this? I thought we
Westerners had a monopoly on spicing our conversations with
quotations from our number one book and the source of our
culture, the *Holy Bible*. But my Chinese students tell me that

they have the same thought in their culture. So what does it mean? It seems to me that there are only two possibilities. One thought would be that many of the quotations in the Bible were universal truths at the time of the writing, spread throughout all the cultures of the time. Perhaps. The only other possible explanation is that the Chinese have had a great deal of Bible teaching in their culture throughout their history, and they use the Bible in their culture far more than the present generation knows.

91

Right-Handed Southpaws

Luke is a southpaw. No doubt about it! He dribbles and shoots the basketball lefty style. He bats and throws the softball lefty style. He wears his watch on the right wrist lefty style. Luke even walks with that slight tilt that is inherent in terminally severe southpaws.

But Luke does not write with his left hand. Not at all! When I demonstrated to the class how I hold the pen, turned the hand upside down, and did my poor imitation of penmanship, Luke didn't even give a sincere effort to try it. He writes with his right hand. Period. Luke is even taking lessons to master the art of Chinese calligraphy – all with his right hand.

Luke is not alone in China. He is not even part of the majority. Right-handed writers are unanimous. No exceptions. Eight thousand students on our campus and not a left-handed writer to be found. Sometimes just being Caucasian and American was more of a conspicuous distinction than I needed, but writing with my left hand was the phenomenon that moved me all the way into the realm of a complete freak. People came from miles around just to watch me write.

When Mary and I visited schools, the students, out of a combination of curiosity and courtesy, asked us for autographs.

We signed anything and everything – notebooks, textbooks, letters from Mom, tee shirts and palms.

Usually those young students were so absorbed in the alien character of the whole situation – Americans in their middle school – that they forgot to notice my upside down left-handed writing. But if someone did notice and would shout above the din the Chinese equivalent of "sinistral," the mild chaos of the moment turned instantaneously into potential danger for all living beings in the fallout zone. Left-handed writing is simply unheard of – even if Luke is a natural born southpaw.

"Why?" you ask.

I will tell you why. I don't know why. Perhaps teachers do force, coerce, rant, rave and punish until innocent southpaw children are permanently converted, but I didn't witness such activity or even hear about it. Rather, it just seemed that no one had ever thought that writing with the left hand was even a possibility. Teachers didn't have to correct it because nobody tried it. It is simply not done.

Is it a cultural thing hidden deep in antiquity somewhere with the origin long forgotten but the tradition living on? Is it a practical thing, preparing students for the right-handed work world in their future? Is it a product of government managed conformity – no one unusual, no one different – just a part of the standard issue uniform?

I don't know the answer to any of those questions. I just know that Luke is a right-handed southpaw.

Early Morning Study

In American schools, we have one approach to reading – quantity. We don't give free pizzas for how much the readers learned. We give free pizza for how many books they covered.

The Chinese have two approaches to reading – quantity and quality. They call it intensive reading and extensive reading. During the educational process, they are taught to read thoroughly, pouring over every word, every phrase and every expression. To accomplish this intensive reading technique, they read aloud.

Do you remember when your second grade teacher said, "I like the way Edith is reading. She doesn't move her mouth. I want all of you to learn to read like Edith and not move your mouth?" Well, your second grade teacher doesn't teach in China.

One of the principal learning strategies for the university students was to read the text aloud as often as needed to grasp all the details. This is a sight to behold.

Imagine the scene – early morning: the sun reflecting off the mountain, the smell of dew on the leaves, every park bench crammed with students reading aloud, oblivious to the people around them and the passers-by. The more energetic ones are walking about punctuating their oral reading with gestures and body movements.

Imagine arriving at 7:20 a.m. for an 8:00 a.m. college class and finding the room already packed with diligent students fervently pouring over their lessons — reading aloud and loudly. I don't think they ever consciously started a volume contest, but they needed to hear themselves, so they read loudly enough to be heard above their neighbor. Of course, the neighbor responded by upping the amps, and soon the room was filled with the delightful sounds of twenty-four students reading their lessons loudly enough to be heard over the din.

Watching all that energy and all that enthusiasm, I was almost reluctant to start class, but when I did stand to say something, the students responded immediately, and the noise came crashing down over us.

After several months away from the place, when I wake up in the middle of the night and my mind wanders to my China life as it frequently does, one of the memories that is sure to flit across the horizon is that of early morning study and a room full of students reading aloud.

Moving the Tombs

Fellow-teacher Aifeng came to class Monday morning with puffy eyes and that haggard look that indicates a tough weekend. I was gracious. I avoided the urge to pry. After all, weekends are private despite our American dose of curiosity.

In class, students read their original poems. Being college students and being Chinese, they had poured themselves into the opportunity to pluck at heartstrings. In other words, they had written quite moving lines, often about family, and they punctuated their readings with pregnant pauses and even appropriate tears.

Aifeng responded appropriately also. She broke out in uncontrollable weeping and had to leave the room. Under those circumstances, I thought I had earned the right to pry. The result was a great study in the clash of the old and the new – traditional China at war with changes.

Aifeng had spent her weekend visiting her hometown. She and her brothers and sisters had been ordered by the government to take care of a piece of family business. A few years before when their father had died, they showed their respect and love – traditional Chinese virtues – by burying him on a small plot on his farm and building a small tomb to his memory

– nothing elaborate, but a gesture of honor, respect, love, and tradition, something families had done in China for centuries. Those tombs are everywhere.

Now, the government explains that with the decreasing land supply and the growing need for food, the tomb had to be moved. They simply cannot occupy the valuable space. Families had a choice – either cremate the remains or find another spot higher up the mountain out of the range of valuable land. Aifeng's family chose the second and had spent the weekend moving their father's remains.

Forget the slogans! Forget the philosophy lectures! Forget the government decrees! When it comes time to move your ancestors' tombs, the worldview you put together while sitting in classes isn't worth too much. At that point, the worldview that counts is the one that you inherited over several generations and that you have made a personal spiritual commitment to.

98

To examine Aifeng's emotions that Monday morning, let's put ourselves into her position, and the position of many Chinese. Suppose for the sake of a valid national reason, the government ordered all cemeteries turned into farmland. Families could reclaim the headstones or they would be destroyed.

At this point, what is the nature of your worldview which will help you make it through the ordeal dry-eyed and composed?

When the Birds Chirp

Our university is a beautiful place. Located on the outskirts of the city, the campus has ample space filled with all sorts of foliage – pine trees, magnolia trees, orange trees, hardwood trees, hedges and bushes, flowers, grass, and clover, and even a walk with a wisteria covered canopy.

To add to all this beauty, the university has built stone benches and tables to form small parks, and the whole campus is centered around a man-made three-acre pond with rock banks.

With all this foliage, there isn't any wild life – no rabbits, no squirrels, and only a rare bird once in awhile to chirp the celebration of the rising sun.

Don't ask, because I don't know why, but apparently, this is the situation all over China. Our students, when watching an American movie, would gasp at the scene of a flock of birds, and then they would ask, "Is this for real?"

They almost couldn't believe me when I explained about squirrels and rabbits pestering students on university campuses in America. It's just too far outside their realm of reference.

Were the birds and animals ever there in the first place? If so, when and where did they go? Will they ever come back?

It's just another mystery of life in wonderfully mysterious China.

Eyeglasses

As soon as you walk into the classroom, you notice it – the unusual number of students wearing glasses – more than seventy percent in any college classroom.

I can only guess at the reasons. Many of the classrooms, libraries and dorm rooms where children spend much of their lives studying are dimly lighted. There is always dust and pollution in the air, which might cause eye infections. One of the first tasks of waking up each morning is to clean the trash out of the corners of the eyes where it has collected during the night.

Perhaps the most obvious reason for so many students in glasses is the sheer volume of reading and studying they have to do – school days from 8:00 a.m. until 9:30 p.m. with assigned study periods – six or six and one-half days a week – ten and one-half months a year. The stress on the eyes is overwhelming!

School officials have recognized the problem and have attempted some solutions. For one thing, eye exercises have been worked into the daily classroom routine. At least a couple of times a day, the class comes to a halt, and the students perform a set of exercises under the supervision of the teacher and the class monitor. The exercises themselves are structured with specific target areas. Using the fingers and thumbs of both hands, students massage their noses, cheekbones, brows and eye sockets. The whole process takes about two or three minutes, and the students treat the whole endeavor with a seriousness which demonstrates that they think it is important.

These eye exercises are a part of the educational scene all the way from kindergarten to the end of high school.

Although I never mastered all the finer points properly, I tried them a couple of times and found them refreshing and relaxing.

I can't help but wonder how many college students would wear glasses if they didn't stop their education a couple of times a day to do relaxing techniques.

The Great Wall

We have the Statue of Liberty. The Chinese have the Great Wall. That ancient and impressive structure makes a statement for every individual about the Chinese spirit. It stands as a testament of industriousness, ingenuity and cooperative effort. It represents the best of who they are as a people.

Most Chinese have never seen the Great Wall. For most of them, visiting the Wall and seeing it in person is a dream pilgrimage – what they would do if they won the lottery and inherited a fortune. They want to go. They dream of going, but they never really expect to get there.

Part of the dream is fueled by one of the most famous statements of Chairman Mao, "To be a complete person, you must visit the Great Wall."

Although most of them have never seen the Great Wall themselves, they can tell you about it. They know all the details – the size and shape and structure, but more importantly, they know the details of the construction – how far the stones were carried, how many people worked on the project, how the stones were lifted into place without the help of machines. They even know how many people died during the building process.

This is who they are. Through the sweat of their brows and the aches in their backs, the Chinese working together on a common project can accomplish anything without tools or machines — just effort applied to a common cause.

This is what the Great Wall means to the person on the street in a village thousands of miles away, too far for them to ever realistically hope of seeing it.

I saw the Great Wall once. When we first arrived in China back in 1988, we began our tourist venture by taking a trip out to the Wall. I was impressed, but that is all. I was merely impressed. After all, I was just a tourist.

In a way, I wish I had waited to see the Great Wall until after I had met my Chinese friends in other parts of the country so that I could have truly appreciated the meaning of the privilege I have had!

Twirling Pens

We strive to produce students who are creative thinkers, then we ignore manifestations of success.

One obvious example is the variety of techniques students develop to help them cope with the tension of the classroom. Some wiggle! Some stretch and yawn. Some crack their joints or even their backs. Some chew gum even when it's contraband. Some take quick naps. Some tap their pencils on their desks.

As usual, expect the Chinese students to combine tradition, grace, skill, art, and uniformity to something as everyday as tension-coping mechanisms. They twirl their pens on their thumbs. I hope you get the picture because I really can't describe it. They lay their pens on their thumbs and twirl them. That's quite a sight to behold – a class full of students deep in thought – pondering the right answer to test questions – formulating a meaningful sentence to put on paper – mesmerized by my lecture (just kidding.) There they sit – thinking and twirling. Although there was a uniformity in the art form, each had a distinctive style. Some could even twirl with either hand.

I must confess that of all the tension coping strategies I have seen during my teaching career, I like pen twirling the best. For one thing, it's silent – not nearly as disruptive as tapping on the desk which is too common in our schools. But beyond that, it shows a sense of accomplishment, a bit of beauty woven into the midst of the day's activities — just another feature of the charm of the Chinese culture.

Christmas Parties

It's always interesting to discover what we Americans export to other countries. Some of our exports serve as a sense of pride for us. Other exports such as cigarettes and pornography bring a sense of shame.

Imagine our surprise when we found that one of our most conspicuous exports to China was Christmas! We weren't ready for that. We had prepared ourselves to spend a bleak December without ceremony or fanfare celebrating in our own private way what our students and colleagues wouldn't understand.

But it didn't happen that way. The season began about as early as it does in the United States, and by the twenty-fifth of December, it had begun to look a lot like Christmas all across town and across the campus. If we missed any of the trappings, we don't know what they were. We had Christmas cards – a bit humorous at times, but cards. We had Santa Claus, decorated trees, Christmas music, wrapping paper and of course, gifts. Because we were the Americans and because we were the teachers, we had lots of gifts – more than four suitcases full when we brought them home.

In the midst of this, the biggest event was the campus-wide Christmas party in the cinema – the huge auditorium seating three thousand. It was jammed – standing room only.

The three-hour program was prepared by the communist student group. It featured singing, dancing, short plays and even a choir.

Early in the planning stage, I was invited to participate as Santa Claus, making an entrance in the middle of a dance routine featuring twelve of my students. I was honored. After searching the city, the students managed to find a Santa Claus suit – extra-large even. Extra-large in Chinese, of course. It came to the middle of my stomach.

A couple of days before the Christmas Eve event, the departmental party leader came to me with a problem. She explained that although the Chinese had learned about some of the ceremonies of Christmas, they had no idea why we even had such a holiday. Since I was going to be on stage anyway as Santa Claus, could I take about ten minutes to explain the meaning of the event?

That's what I did. I presented the Christmas story to those three thousand students and professors packed into the cinema. It was one of the biggest thrills of my life.

We might ask ourselves why the concept of Christmas exploded so vigorously across the country if they don't know the origin. Is it their desire to imitate anything Western? Is it just a matter of opportunistic merchants taking advantage of a sales gimmick? Whatever the reason, I get rather excited thinking about the explosion of the rites of Christmas and wonder if someday soon there could even be such an explosion of understanding the reason for Christmas.

108

Classmates

In a Chinese high school, the classroom is assigned to the students, and the teachers move every hour. Isn't that an unusual twist which makes a great deal of sense? Instead of having two thousand students running through the halls to get to the next class as we do in the United States, they have only teachers making the trek. It surely saves a lot of chaos.

But there is another serendipitous feature of this practice. The students in the classroom are together throughout the entire school day. They sit in the same seats surrounded by the same people and interact almost completely with students in that one familiar group. Frequently, those classes are formed during the students' first year in high school, and they spend all their time with the same classmates for the next three years. Of course, at the high school level, these are still rather large groups — as many as fifty or sixty. Nevertheless, when they spend that much time together, they do develop close ties, and the concept of classmate is synonymous with the concept of friendship. High school classmates are friends for life. In fact, many university students told me that their closest friend in the world was their high school seatmate. In other words, two students were randomly selected to sit next to each other for their high school classes, and as a result, they come together in a lifetime bond.

I find this as something of a contrast with the American educational experience. For whatever it is we are trying to accomplish, friendship is not one of them. Our system is designed to produce alienation and loneliness. For years, I have talked about the loneliness of many high school students; often I preached to deaf ears – even to students who won't admit that they are lonely. But in China, I saw the contrast.

This method of organization seemed valuable for carrying out some other arrangement. For one thing, high school students are forbidden to date. It is simply not allowed, and violators are punished severely. The classroom structure, on the other hand, allows for some cross-gender friendships which permit the children to learn something about the opposite sex. The classroom structure also enables the students to form study buddies and to encourage and motivate each other. With this kind of classroom identity, students were prompted to do their best for the good of the team as well as for personal gain.

This idea of group structure is carried into the university as well. When people arrive as first year students, they are assigned to a class group, and for the next four years they have all classes together, study together, have outings together, and even live together. In other words, they become inseparable with about twenty-five other students for four years. Thus, when a Chinese person tells you that someone was a classmate, remember that speaks of a profound relationship.

Michael Jordan

What is an icon? A human form larger than life? An international symbol for reverence and perfection? Why, it's Michael Jordan!

Everywhere it's Michael Jordan. In the cities, in the remotest countryside villages – whether they were elementary children with only two sentences of English or university students studying for advanced degrees, the first question asked was always the same. "Do you know Michael Jordan?"

But it wasn't the words of the question which made it special. It was the tone – the awe, the respect, the sense that we were speaking about the ultimate of America.

With the same spirit, children of all ages from four years to sixty wore the famous "Bulls 23" shirts with a dignity which suggested that they were advertising their approval of a way of life.

I can't explain all this. I have no idea why Michael Jordan is an icon in China. Although the Chinese do play some basketball, the sport isn't really an obsession like soccer or ping-pong. Although they do get replays of NBA games, these are shown on TV at unusual times and shouldn't have that large an audience.

So what is the magic? What is the appeal? Why is Michael Jordan the most famous American throughout China?

I don't know the answer, but I must admit that I am always amazed to see what we Americans export, whether intentionally or unintentionally.

A Dream of
Red Mansions

Exam time:
  Name a significant literary work by a British author.
  Name a significant literary work by a Russian author.
  Name a significant literary work by a French author.
  Name a significant literary work by an African author.
  Name a significant literary work by a Chinese author.
  How did you do? Let me guess. At best, you got four out of
five. Why is it that most of us have never heard of a Chinese
novel, and could never hope to name even one Chinese novelist?

  We might say that it is written in another language and has
to be translated, but we know the works of the Russians.

  Let's admit it. Most of us have simply ignored Chinese literature. It isn't that we have made a decision about its quality or
value. We have just never thought of it.

  Let me assure you that our omission does not go unnoticed
among the Chinese. They are painfully aware that we don't
know their literature. With a culture as old as theirs and a
written language as old as theirs, they have never had a Nobel
Prize winner in literature, a tidbit of news residing in the minds
of every educated person.

Let me offer you a tip. If you are interested in China at all, or if you ever think that you will meet a Chinese person visiting America, or if you think you may someday visit China yourself, do something noble. Run down to your library and check out the novel, *A Dream of Red Mansions* by Cao XueQin.

It is a grand epic style novel of two volumes written about 250 years ago. With themes of love, life, class struggles and honor and integrity, it represents the Chinese spirit. Most of them will tell you that this is the classic that rises above all others — the place to start your study of Chinese literature.

Through reading the novel, you will be able to develop an understanding for the culture that you couldn't hope to grasp by reading sociology or history books. If you ever have any contact with China whatsoever, you will be happy that you have read this novel.

Besides if you ever mention it to a Chinese person, you will have a friend for life.

Correction Tape

Problem: How do you erase a sentence on your essay once you have already written it in ink?

Solution: You stick some cellophane tape across it, push it down securely, and rip it off carrying the unwanted sentence away, never to bother you again.

Isn't this ingenious? When I first saw the rolls of cellophane tape in the students' pencil boxes, I wondered what they were for. I hadn't seen them use the tape to repair anything or to attach anything, and I wondered why they needed so much tape.

I assigned the first essay to be written in class, and I discovered the use. This was correction tape, designed particularly for that purpose. Soon the practice of erasing by ripping the tape away was so common throughout the class that I soon forgot that it was new to me, and I had never seen this method used anywhere else in the world.

Now it is just another aspect of teaching in China – unusual, strange, but all part of the experience.

Monitors

Annie needed more confidence in herself. She had planned to study art, but because of her exam scores during Black July, she had been assigned to be an English major. She was as good as the other students, but she didn't know it. I had to force her to talk to me, but when I did manage to encourage her to speak English, I found her thoughts worthwhile and informative.

One day she handed me her homework assignment, an original essay arguing a point. As I read it that night, I realized that part of it, if not all of it, was plagiarized. I couldn't prove my accusation. I had no way to build my case, and I had no intention of doing the research required to substantiate my suspicions. That is just something you learn by some kind of a teacher's sixth sense. After forty years of doing this, I just know when a student has plagiarized.

I didn't want to create an international incident, and I didn't want to discourage Annie anymore than she already was, but I had to deal with the problem. Although it was already 9:00 p.m. with only an hour and one-half left until "lights out," I called the dormitory, and Annie said she would be right over.

She did come. She came quickly, and she came contritely, but she brought Ellen with her. Annie knew that she was in trouble. She knew what she had done, and I am sure that she had come expecting harsh consequences. That's why she brought Ellen.

Ellen is the class monitor. Let me explain that. When Annie came to our university and was put into the English department, she was assigned into group 972 – a group of twenty-five students who have all their classes together and who actually live with each other in the dormitory. Shortly after the forming of the group, students in 972 elected Ellen as their monitor.

This is another distinctive feature of Chinese education. All groups or all classes have a designated monitor.

What a great idea! These monitors work as secretaries, runners, communication channels, organizers, visionaries and Mother Superiors. They are invaluable to teachers. If you need to hand back papers, use the monitor. If you need to collect money for a movie night, use the monitor. If you want to send a message to selected class members, use the monitor.

They are also invaluable to the group. Their position is seen as a remarkable marriage of service and leadership. All the while they are tending to the mundane needs of their classmates, they are earning respect as the leader – someone to be admired and followed. Although I did not have enough experience to make a scientific conclusion, I noticed that the group frequently took on the personality of the monitor.

On the night I called Annie about the paper, I guess I should have expected Ellen to come. Her classmate was in trouble. More importantly, her subject was in trouble. As the leader, Ellen took it personally. She was as involved as Annie.

As is often the case in such situations, the outcome of our meeting was not nearly as severe as I had built myself to expect.

Without any accusation from me, Annie admitted what she had done, and I realized that she was not motivated by laziness, but by fear. She had actually worked harder to find the material to copy than some of her classmates who had done the assignment correctly. She copied because she was afraid that her own thought processes and language skills would be inadequate.

She didn't need criticism or punishment. She needed encouragement. I gave it to her. She proposed to do the assignment correctly. I agreed, and we parted amicably.

All the while, Ellen, monitor, leader, servant, friend and Mother Superior, held Ellen's hand and smiled heartily with the outcome as if it were a personal victory for her.

The Sports Meet

Interscholastic sports don't play a major role in Chinese universities! No stadiums dominating the landscape, no star jocks walking around the campus, no big games, no fight songs, no mascots, no cheerleaders.

We heard that our university had a basketball team, but we never could find out when or where they played, so obviously, it wasn't all that important to anybody.

Thus, the sports event of the year was an intramural affair – a three-day campus-wide track and field meet complete with opening and closing exercises featuring a cast of thousands, parades, ceremonies and rituals. Even without the races and contests, it was an exciting time. As an example of how important the event was, the university dismissed classes for three days, an unusual turn of events for us.

We didn't need any encouragement to attend. By May, we were so hungry for sports stuff that we were the first in the stands and the last to leave. All three days! We spent our time cheering and cheering, and we had good reason. Our students, the English majors, are not distinguished for their athletic prowess. All the really top athletes, both male and female, came from the political science department. That's just an isolated fact for which I have no commentary.

In addition to spending three days bumping into our students and colleagues in a more relaxed and playful environment, we learned some language. The Chinese equivalent to "rah, rah" is literally translated, "Put oil in the machine." Isn't that delightful! There we sat, cheering Kevin to a fourth place in the four hundred meter run, Lucy to fifth place in the long jump, Linda to a third place in the five thousand meter run, Tommy to a second place in the three thousand meter run and literally encouraging them to put oil in their machine. I have recently attended some basketball games where I thought that message might be appropriate, and I had to stifle the urge to yell, "Jia you." Unfortunately, it doesn't have the same catchy rhythm in English as it does in Chinese.

There were even special races for faculty and staff which attracted runners of all ages, including the academic vice-president. Even with this kind of participation, every athlete in every event was treated as if he or she was important, and participation was taken seriously. The starters and judges carried out their responsibilities with a tone of respect for the participant and a spirit of fair play. Regardless of their native abilities, or lack thereof, students had the opportunity of being treated as if they were athletes, at least once during the year.

I find it interesting that we Americans sometimes project the image that we are the fitness buffs. The Chinese never gave me that impression until the sports meet, when as many as forty-percent of our students demonstrated skill and conditioning for a moment of glory.

Daryl and Teri were coming to see us. That's Dr. Daryl McCarthy, CEO of Cooperative Studies, and his wife, Teri, Director of Faculty Development for the organization.

SRO at the Wedding

Although Daryl and Teri have been husband and wife for a few years, they haven't been at it for forty years, so we still think of them as newlyweds.

Because their scheduled visit was to coincide with my weekly lecture in the big hall at the library, Mary and I decided to combine the two events into a simulated learning experience. We would hold an American wedding so our students and friends could see one of our basic cultural events.

As usual, Daryl and Teri were good sports about it all – with emphasis on Teri. Never has a bride walked down the aisle more creatively dressed. She wore a beautiful gown constructed from one of Mary's night gowns and an accompanying table cloth.

Our students served as bridesmaids and groom attendants. A visiting American couple, Jim and Ruth Youngsman from Washington, were parents of the groom, while another couple from Illinois, Bill and Carol Schmidtgall, were parents of the bride. Cooperative Studies teachers, Scott and Janelle Higgins, were the featured singers. Our special student, Janet, read a Shakespearian sonnet; Mary read from First Corinthians, and I performed the ceremony using the text of the wise and foolish builders as a base.

It was a fun evening – a memorable event, and all the Chinese present – students, teachers and visitors were generous with their praise and gratitude.

But in the midst of all this activity, the real spectacle was the crowd. The big hall in the library where the event was scheduled to take place seats about three hundred and fifty. When the powers that be anticipated the excitement of the night, they knew that there would be a crowd, so they negotiated for a lecture room in another building with a capacity for seven hundred and fifty.

The seats were occupied at least an hour before we were to begin. Next, teachers, students and general public crammed into the aisles and stood at the front and the back. There was also a crowd surrounding the outside of the building peering through the open windows, pushing, and shoving for their places.

The major challenge of the whole night was getting the bride down the aisle and getting the newly married couple out when it was all over. This mass of people gives new meaning to the term SRO. SRO crowds I can manage. What do you do when the standing room is all occupied?

Although the wedding was the biggest draw we had, we did see those kinds of crowds regularly. They came in almost that kind of quantity for each of the weekly lectures and for some other special lectures around campus. It does stroke the ego to see folks standing outside, crowded around open windows to try to catch a hint of my wisdom. But in reality, it is probably just another feature of a highly populated world.

Black Arm Patches

$\mathbf{J}$ulie came to class the second week wearing a black patch pinned to her sleeve. Because she seemed to be a bright girl who liked to talk, because she sat on the front row, and because we had a few minutes to kill, I decided to learn something about the culture, so I asked Julie about her patch. Mistake! Through quantities of tears, she told me that her grandfather had just died.

From that pit of awkwardness, which we teachers sometimes dig for ourselves, I did the only thing I could think of. I reached out and held her hand as she wept in her sorrow.

But I did learn something about the culture from the experience – lessons in fact – some overt and some more serendipitous.

First, I learned that grandparents die in China as well as in the United States. In fact, in my twenty-five years of college teaching, I have helped many students mourn the loss of a grandparent. It frequently happens to people that age. During our year in China, fourteen of my one hundred twenty-five students lost a grandparent.

I also learned that death causes sorrow to those left. Although I had never really believed them, I had heard comments that life can't be worth much to people who live in a country with a billion population. Not true. Human life is human life – precious to all of us. Those students suffered a real hurt when they lost a grandparent, and their grief process required the necessary time. Although they only wore the patches about a week, they mourned way past the time of the public announcement.

But the other lesson is a far more profound one which I am still trying to process fully. After the students removed the black patches and they moved away from the sympathy of their classmates, they came to our apartment to visit us because each student had some deep question about living and dying which they couldn't discuss in any other setting.

These were all good students – among the top five percent in the country. They were widely read and schooled in both Chinese traditional philosophy and communism. I don't know what they learned in all those classes, but I did come to realize that there comes a time in life when government theories, economic principles and moral philosophy is not enough. The death of a grandparent is too personal for any of that. At times like these, we must reach deeper into our being and find the spiritual fiber that holds us together, even when we are Chinese students who once memorized a creed which says that religion is the opium of the people.

Such creeds lose their meaning when it comes time to wear a black arm patch.

The Smile Behind the Hand

I confess. I like manners – any public display of manners – particularly by students. I don't care if they are contrived, memorized or coerced by authority.

The problem with teaching in China was that I didn't know whether the behavior was brought on by a sense of manners or something else.

One such demonstration was the feminine smile. Frequently when they smiled and especially when they felt the smile might break out into outright laughter, the girls would hide their mouths behind their hands.

How do I describe it? Cute? Coy? Flirty? I'm not sure, but I often found the gesture refreshing and rewarding. I would make a stab at humor – always a risky venture in a cross-cultural setting – and an added risk in a classroom where humor is outside the expected context. For whatever reason – embarrassment, sympathy, pity, or perhaps an even natural response to the funny, students would sometimes laugh. What a reinforcement that was – to think that the foreigner could make them laugh. Some guys would laugh vigorously, in fact.

Some girls laughed heartily too, but they put their hands in front of their faces as they did. That was one of the highest tributes I received during my whole year – to watch those hands cover the smile.

What is the cultural background of this? I don't know. I do know that, traditionally, Chinese girls had been taught the fine art of femininity – demure, shy, coy — only to be seen, never to be heard. Never loud, never demonstrative, and I did notice that the girls who had grown up in the more traditional homes were the first to lift the hands.

Did they put their hands up because there is something unseemly about showing teeth in public? When they pick their teeth after a meal, they do use both hands – one doing the work while the other serving as a curtain, so maybe there is something about public display of teeth in the manner code.

Whatever the reason, the girls accomplished something with their gesture. They might have covered their mouths to hide the smiles, but they couldn't cover the laughter in their eyes, and those dancing eyes communicated so effectively.

Beijing Opera and Backstreet Boys

I asked my students to write essays about the generation gap in China. They told me there was one, and it often provokes heated discussions around three issues: spending money, dress and music.

Isn't it nice to know that we aren't all that different? Or maybe those are universal themes of debate between generations, anytime, anyplace.

Throughout history and around the world, how many families have encountered tension because of the music the children chose to enjoy?

The classic music of China is embodied in an art form called Beijing Opera. Although there are variations of this in other parts of the country, it is still called Beijing Opera.

As a complete art form, it has not only the qualities of music but it also includes costuming, set decorations, staging and body language. It is all founded in tradition, and it is quite complex, requiring years of study for full understanding.

Until just recently, there were no women actors in Beijing Opera, so all roles were played by men. Each costume, complete with mask, tells a story of its own. There are good people and bad people, fair people and mean people, powerful people and weak people, all communicated by the costume and mask. The audience can identify the villains and heroes as soon as they walk on stage.

The music itself is classic Chinese. The instruments are mostly stringed affairs which don't look anything like any kind of Western instruments.

Although I can't describe it, the singing in Beijing Opera is distinctive too. As a musical illiterate, I would describe it as high-pitched wailing, but it is unforgettable.

All of this, the costuming, the music, and the staging, requires acquired taste. Chinese youth don't enjoy Beijing Opera just because they are Chinese. This reality is a topic of concern for the older generation. Is this a dying art form, a part of the culture from ancient times now on the endangered species list?

Our students who took an elective course in Beijing Opera volunteered to come over to our apartment and explain the rules and the rituals and interpretations as we watched Beijing Opera on television. I don't know whether they came because they enjoyed the opera or because they enjoyed telling us what they knew; but they came often, and we had a delightful time watching together.

Of course, when our lesson in classical music was over, they walked back to their dormitories with their ears glued to their pocket radios tuned to the latest rendition from the Backstreet Boys who are just as popular in China as they are in the United States.

I think they were listening to the Backstreet Boys. They might have been listening to contemporary Chinese rock and roll. I really can't tell the difference.

130

Courtship in the Moonlight

The Chinese paraphrase of a Tennyson line would read, "Spring is the season when young men's fancies lightly turn to thoughts of exams." With the emphasis on exam-driven education, the young people are encouraged to forget about romance and concentrate on their studies.

During the high school years, this is mandated. High school students are not allowed to date. It is as simple as that. Of course, in the typical fashion of people that age, some break the rules and engage in a bit of boy-girl relationships, but they are punished if they are caught and even threatened with expulsion.

At the university, some students maintained that dating was still against the rules. Others suggested that it wasn't against the rules, but it was discouraged by the adults in their lives including parents as well as teachers. They just didn't have time to concentrate on their studies and engage in romantic activity simultaneously.

The result of this attitude was that these intelligent, wise young people came across as rather naïve in cross-gender relationships. We would tease them about having a boyfriend or girlfriend much as we would tease eighth graders in the United States. They would act embarrassed, admit to the charge, and make us swear to secrecy. If we saw them together, it would usually be late in the evening, walking around the campus in the moonlight enjoying each other's company and conversation.

Of course, these are university students, and some did carry the relationship further than that. At least that is what we were told, but we never saw it firsthand because they hide that kind of activity from the school authorities and from their parents.

Most of our students assured us that there would be plenty of time for courting and choosing a mate after they had finished their studies and had become active in their professions. Just to help them stay focused, the government does not allow them to marry until the age of twenty-three.

132

Badminton Break

Question: In a tea drinking country like China, what do the people do during the mid-morning coffee break?

Answer: They go outside in pairs and hit a badminton bird back and forth.

Although I never participated personally, I found break time therapeutic and refreshing. I was invigorated just walking across the university campus watching it all happen. The badminton break gave them exercise to lots of body parts – legs and arms and heart. I am sure the stretching and limbering made them feel much better.

The activity is portable. All they need are two rackets, a bird, and some open space. They just imagined the court and net.

The activity is available to everybody – young and old, men and women. It doesn't matter how they match up because you can't tell much difference between the skillful and the clumsy when you are playing with an imaginary net. Who's keeping score anyway?

Nothing earthshaking about this. No cultural commentary or analysis. Just another example of the delightful activities the Chinese fill their lives with.

Grandma and Grandpa

Grandparent is not a term describing kinship. Oh, no! That is the name of the office – an office of nobility which carries special privileges and responsibilities.

Frankly, I rather envy the people who hold the office in China. In many families, Grandma and Grandpa get the delightful obligation of being principal caretaker of the child.

This comes about through a whole collection of circumstances.

One of those is movement. Chinese families just don't move as much as American families, so, frequently, several generations will live their lives in the same city. Thus, grandparents do get some responsibility through proximity.

In other families where the parents have had to move away for professional reasons, they often send the child back home to stay with grandparents until the child is old enough to start to school. This is because both parents are required to work, and daycare is not often in the picture.

They have no choice but to use the grandparent. We have several friends who are in this situation. As young professional educators, they are actively teaching while their child is staying with grandparents a four-hour train ride away. Of course, the parents go to see their child as often as possible, but frequently, that isn't often enough.

Last year, one of our graduate students left her three month old baby with Grandma while she came to work on her master degree. In other words, Mom parted from her daughter in September, spent the month of February with the child, and did not see her again until July. Mom often came to class with tears in her eyes and an explanation. She was thinking about her baby – a baby she would not know for the first year of her life.

Another circumstance which contributes to the grandparent office is retirement. Workers often retire in their mid-50's, and nursing homes or assisted living homes for the elderly are not only non-existent in China, but the concept is unthinkable.

"Why do you throw your old people away?" we were asked often by a wide variety of people ranging from high school students to retirees.

Although I found the wording to be a little harsh, I still had difficulty answering the question to their satisfaction. This is what they think we do, and I couldn't explain it away.

In China, many retirees have a function. They fill the noble office of grandparent, and they stay active and useful completing their duties. This is an accepted role.

Grandparents accept it. Parents accept it. Society accepts it. But most importantly, the children themselves accept it. Often I saw this picture. Grandparent and child walking hand in hand, exploring, relaxing, chatting and bonding, and the scene filled me with feelings of delight and envy.

Morning Exercises and Sunday Inspections

"This university has too many rules!" How often I have listened to students around the world register this complaint! Regardless of the number of regulations, they still think there are too many.

It was fun to hear the Chinese students complain, and I suppose they had a reason. They did live with certain structures and rules. Most of the students have between twenty and twenty-five hours of classes a week with homework assignments added to the load. Students complete specified classes with very few options, even in choosing instructors. Students are assigned their classmates with whom they take all classes, and they are even assigned roommates. Dating is officially discouraged, and all students have to be in their beds when lights go off each night at 10:30 p.m.

All students are placed in work units and have the duty of keeping a specific area of the campus clean. All freshmen come to the university three weeks early for required military training consisting of marching and non-weapon drills.

But in discussions, we heard no criticism of these structures. Instead the students concentrated their frustration on two rules – morning exercises and Sunday inspections.

After having gone to bed at 10:30 p.m., the students are rousted out at 6:00 a.m. and must greet the new day with required exercises. Although there is some variety, often the exercise consisted of running a mile.

Students did not enjoy the morning exercises. Even those who would have exercised anyway and even did more than was required did not appreciate the rule. They thought that such a restriction was an infringement on their basic rights as students. Some apparently cheated. They were apprehended, rebuked, and punished. On two or three occasions, girls came to class crying because they had been punished for cutting corners on the morning exercise requirement.

The other source of complaining was the mandatory Sunday inspection. With eight people in a dormitory room, junk accumulates; so the university had rules – rules for how many shoes they could have, rules for how many clothes they could have, rules for how many stuffed animals they could have. In other words, there were rules requiring order and tidiness.

138

In order to make sure the rules were fulfilled, inspection teams came on Sunday. According to the student reports, these teams were thorough, noting penalties of even the most minor infractions. If a room failed inspection, the occupants were punished and even fined.

This process provoked the greatest number of complaints. Students debated the requirement at such gatherings as English corner and English-only club meetings. As something of an outsider, I enjoyed listening to the arguments. They made me feel at home. During my twenty-five years of university teaching, I have discovered that students have to complain about something.

I would assume that the university officials, being typical university officials, hole up in some office somewhere and chuckle about the complaints. "If we can keep them focused on the injustice of morning exercises and Sunday inspections, we can add all the course requirements we want to."

Lincolns and Beggars

ny trip downtown provides an education in itself. While
you are fishing in your pocket for a coin to give to a beggar, you are distracted by someone driving by in a Lincoln Town car. The paradoxes are abundant.

We have friends from several sectors of life – teachers, administrators, doctors, merchants, traveling salesmen, factory managers, TV producers and journalists. Except for the variety in their work duties, their lives are rather similar. They work six days a week; they live in apartments in six-story buildings; they live on a diet of rice, vegetables, and fish; they ride bicycles because they can't afford cars.

There just doesn't seem to be too much difference in living standards among the giant middle class. Yet, the trip downtown reminds us that regardless of the economic principles or government structures, there are still extremes on both ends of the continuum.

I don't know how people get to be beggars, and I don't know how people make the money to buy a Lincoln, but it happens, even in China.

Fruit and Flowers

"Dr. Schimmels, I teach in the biology department. I have written a paper to deliver at a conference. Could you help me with it?"

"Sure." I was pleased for the opportunity to pay back the university for everyone's kindness to us.

She came to the apartment, and we worked on the paper for about an hour. She brought a case of oranges for our trouble.

"Cliff, I'm translating some poetry, and I have difficulty with some idioms."

"Sure, I would love to help you because we are friends."

He came to the apartment; we worked fifteen minutes. He brought a beautiful flower arrangement for our trouble.

I have hundreds of those stories, and every one of them embarrasses me. I like to give. That's part of my nature. That's one reason why we went to China – to give them what we know – our knowledge, our perspective, our experience. We had lots of opportunities to give during the year. And we gave a lot and often, but we are still in their debt because every time we gave to somebody, that person gave back to us far more than we could ever give them.

Students would drop by with fruit just because they thought of us when they were shopping. After they had been home for a visit, they brought us a sample of their mother's special goodies. Friends and colleagues stopped by for a word of counsel, and they brought leeche fruit, or a citrus fruit we had never tasted, or pears, or baked sweet potatoes. On my birthday, I got ten flower arrangements and six cakes!

The one lesson we learned during our year at the university is that you can't outgive the Chinese. There is no need trying. You may as well relax and learn to live with their hospitality.

Pedicabs, Taxis, Busses and Trains

This is simply my commentary on public transportation. Because automobiles are a luxury way beyond the dreams of most , the Chinese depend on public transportation to get them to where their feet and their bicycles can't take them.

In my opinion, public transportation is not a limitation of freedom, but an extension of freedom. What a joy to go downtown to eat or to go to a concert or to go to the dragon festival and not have to worry about negotiating your car through the traffic and the crowds and finding a place to park free from concerns of vandalism and tickets. I love public transportation.

Riding the pedicabs is a little tricky. Most of these operators would be frightened to speak one word of English. Some of them probably can't even speak Putonghua, the official language of China. Nevertheless, they are enterprising businessmen. Although they had never seen anyone as large as we are, they seemed to welcome the challenge, and they would gesture for us to get into their cabs so they could pedal us about the city. We didn't ride the pedicabs though, partly because we didn't know how to communicate and partly because we felt sorry for them.

Taxis were different. Through gestures, grunts, limited words and written instructions, we always managed to tell the taxi driver where we wanted to go. The drivers always responded quickly and courteously, and they charged us the price on the box and were thrilled when we left a tip. In any city we visited, we were always pleased with the taxi service.

I like the public buses because they come with both a driver and a conductor who not only collects the fares but also leans out the window and yells the destination to the people standing on the street. During rush hour, which may come at anytime of the day or night, the conductors play a little game of seeing how many people they can cram aboard. We're not talking of square feet here. We're talking of inches and fractions of inches. In fact, these magicians of space encourage the crowd to exhale in unison so we could make room for just two more. Actually, I just made that part up, but they did yell something during the cramming process encouraging us to make ourselves smaller.

The good news was that you could always get off at your stop. Regardless of how many folks were crowded between you and the door, the conductor would simultaneously shout at the driver and direct the crowd until you were safely at your destination.

Chinese trains are convenient, too. They come through frequently, and they are almost always on time. On the trains, you have four options depending on how much you want to pay and what is available. Fourth class is called hard seats, and that's what they are – hordes of people crowded onto benches. Third class is called soft seats, and these are nice – almost as comfortable as some airplane seats. Second class is called hard sleeper – six hard bunks in an open compartment. First class is called soft sleeper – four comfortable bunks in a closed compartment.

Any venture away from home caused me to conclude that the Chinese are on the move. That statistic of a billion people becomes significant when you think that you can almost count that many in the waiting room of the train station. They are traveling somewhere, but fortunately for the sake of their roads and pocketbooks, they can get there by public transportation.

Christina
and M&M's

I thought Christina did not like me. Actually, I thought
Christina hated me. The signs were all there. She sat in the
back as far away from me as she could get. She never looked at
me – never visited our apartment with her classmates. When I
asked her to write, she scribbled a few sentences and turned
her paper in, basically incomplete.

I tried to establish rapport, but I failed; so I just accepted
the obvious reality that Christina did not like me. Maybe it was-
n't personal. Maybe she just didn't like any foreigners.

In April with the school year three-fourths gone, Jared, a
young man from Lee University, came to help us for a few
weeks. Among his other endeavors to establish relationships
with students and to speak contemporary English, he entered
their sports world in such things as playground basketball and
soccer. But he also played ping-pong with the Chinese students.
Being a good athlete, Jared not only held his own with them at
their game, but he was beating the boys regularly. They com-
plained to me. They didn't much appreciate this American beating them at ping-pong, and they even accused him of cheating.

One day Jared came back to the apartment, and the look
on his face communicated that he was not particularly happy
with life.

"What's wrong?" I put on my sympathy tone.

"I just got beat in ping-pong." He was dejected.

"Badly?" I asked, trying hard to keep from chuckling.

"Slaughtered," he sighed.

"By whom?" I asked with hidden glee.

"Christina," he told me as he dropped his voice.

The next day I assembled a rather large bag of M&M's, waited for a lull in the class, walked all the way back to Christina, placed the bag on the desk, and said simply, "This is for beating Jared."

I didn't even notice her expression, but the next day I was standing in the hall between classes talking to a large group of students when an animated Christina came pushing through the crowd.

"Thank you so much for the sweets," she exclaimed. "I shared them with my roommates. They were delicious."

After that Christina looked at me in class, stopped me in the hall to talk, and came to the apartment for conversation. We talked a great deal about her ping-pong skills. She was good, almost good enough to try out for the Olympics, and she had met one of the national stars.

I planned a short skit for one of my lectures in the large hall in the library, and Christina took on the responsibility of a speaking part – speaking in English in front of three hundred and fifty students. I was proud of her.

When I was preparing to leave at the end of the year, Christina wrote me a four-page letter.

Christina didn't hate me. She didn't even dislike me. But we spent three-fourths of a year with her being afraid of me – intimidated, ashamed, reticent and non-participatory. How often we misjudge the motives of others.

Fortunately, Christina and I managed to jump the hurdle in our relationship – all because of a bag of M&M's. But I still must wonder how often we deprive ourselves of a close fellowship with someone simply because we misread the signs.

Bicycles, Motorchcles and the Front Gate

When I was a school principal, all my rules made sense, at least to me. Now that I am no longer in that business, I wonder how so many silly policies get instituted.

One of the distinguishing features of the Chinese university is the wall which surrounds it. Of course, because there is a protective wall, there is also a gate where all people going in and out must pass under the scrutiny of the guards who are enforcing the policies of the front gate.

One of the policies is that all students, teachers and staff must wear the university pin at all times. That policy makes sense. That way the guards can recognize who belongs so that they keep out unwanted visitors. In fact, I liked the policy, or I did until I forgot my pin one night and was held hostage by the new guard on duty until some teachers came to rescue me.

But the policy that confuses me is the one about the bicycles and motorcycles. Bicycle riders must dismount and walk their bicycles through the gate. This policy even probably makes sense when the riders pass through the small pedestrian gate, but I didn't see the wisdom when the larger gates swing open. Although this might seem minor, it is, in fact, quite serious to the officials. When the students would forget to dismount, the guards would chase them down and write them tickets. But the motorcycle policy is different. While the bicycle riders are walking their machines through the gate, the motorcycle riders throttle down and ride right on by.

I wonder why that is? Why are there two sets of policies for the same gate? I asked several people, but I never got an answer. Oh well, maybe all of my rules didn't make that much sense either.

Twenty-One Channels

When we went to China in 1988, we had one small television in the whole dormitory, and our choices were limited to two stations.

Ten years later, there is at least one TV in almost every home with a twenty-one channel hook-up and a remote control to facilitate surfing. You will have to decide if this is progress.

The twenty-one channels offer a wide variety of options for all tastes. As in the United States, there are national networks and local stations. The national networks, called CCTV, come out of Beijing and feature standard TV fare – sports, news, variety shows, movies and soap operas.

One channel is all sports; another is weather; another provides a continuous updating of the stock market; another is programmed by the military, and yet another features an almost steady diet of Beijing Opera.

To my unsophisticated eye, the Chinese programming seemed to be rather well done. I was particularly impressed with some of the special variety programs featuring singing and dancing and acting. With elaborate costumes, hundreds of people on stage, and such technology as blinking lights and revolving stages, some of the production numbers were about the most magnificent I have ever seen. They were truly production numbers.

Yet, despite all this progress, the Chinese still import major portions of their programs from such places as Japan, Europe, and particularly, America.

One Saturday night, eight of those twenty-one channels featured an American-made movie. Although they sometimes show the movie in English, most of the time the Chinese translations have been dubbed in, and they are quite skillful at this. The readers are good at imitating the expressions and even the voices of the original actors. Try to imagine watching James Stewart open his mouth and speak Chinese in his distinctive halting style. Or better yet, imagine Sylvester Stallone speaking Chinese.

My problem with this is that the movies shown on the twenty-one channels would not be my choice of representative American entertainment.

150   It always amazes me to see what we export and to realize that sometimes we export our worst instead of our best.

Of course, this does provide a couple of new topics for dinner table conversation around the lazy Susan and fried tofu. If students spend so much time watching TV, will they forget how to read? Will watching all that violence on those American-made movies have any kind of impact on the children's moral development?

I wonder if the Chinese parents are always happy with all that progress.

Football in the Dust

I hear that people laugh at genius. Maybe that is why they laughed at me when I asked Teri McCarthy to bring a football when she came to see us.

"Why do you need a football? How is that going to help you teach English? Why don't you ask for textbooks and educational journals?"

Little did they know! That football became one of the learning highlights of the year. Interest peaked as soon as I brought it to class. Everybody, girls and guys alike, wanted to handle and inspect this strange foreign object which represents one facet of America. About the only football activity they had ever seen was what they grabbed from the few scenes in the movie, Forrest Gump, but they knew it was important to Americans, and that made it important to them.

The guys pleaded with me to teach them the game that very afternoon, and I gleefully agreed. The first lesson was an ego boost. They couldn't throw the football. Some of them – the more gifted athletes – learned to catch it after several attempts of trial and error. But not a single one of them learned to throw it. Those strapping young heroes of the soccer field and the basketball court couldn't throw the football. It still amazes me to discover those little tidbits of culture that we don't readily see, but obviously the over-arm motion of throwing a football or a baseball is a culturally learned skill. The Chinese, even the better athletes, couldn't do it.

With me throwing for both sides, I explained the rules, and all of a sudden a contest broke out. I am not sure what we played. It looked a bit like touch football; it looked a bit like rugby; and it looked a great deal like chaos; but the players seemed to understand the rules, although I didn't. We played for two hours, laughing and screaming all the while.

The next day the freshmen guys approached me with football fever. I showed them the ball, and they contacted Mrs. Huang, their teacher, about turning this into an English learning project.

They went to the library and researched fully, learning the rules and regulations. They acquired some lime from the maintenance crew, and they marked off an official-sized football field on the soccer field. This was an interesting sight. Soccer fields in that part of China have no grass. Let me state that again for emphasis. Soccer fields have no grass — completely barren. So here was an official football field laid out in the dust of the soccer field.

Individual classes came to the new attraction to learn the rules and play the game. That provided another interesting sight because foreign language classes are composed of five guys and nineteen girls, some of whom weigh as much as seventy pounds.

For three days, I was the honored coach teaching the game to five guys and nineteen girls. We had a blast, and we learned English. The next time they watched *Forrest Gump*, they knew touchdowns and runbacks and goal lines and helmets – words usually not in their textbooks.

Handwriting

Anytime you visit a home with a child, you have to sit patiently through a recital of the child's talent.

In Tennessee, the children are dragged reluctantly to center stage and asked to sing their ABC Song or their rendition of a Garth Brooks' number or some such song.

In Ukraine, the children have to dance for the visitors.

In China, the proud parents bring out the drawing books. Isn't that an interesting window into a culture? Drawing and handwriting are still valued talents and a source of pride for parents. The children are taught quite young such aspects as perspectives, balance and form. Sometimes, they draw pictures. Sometimes, they draw the Chinese characters.

Families rush to the shops to buy the special brushes and inks the children need to practice their handwork, and the results are often displayed all over the house. In short, good penmanship is an accepted virtue.

Many people continue to practice calligraphy throughout life. If our university students had any extra time, they would often take writing lessons. On warm days the parks are filled with people, tablets in hand, drawing and writing. From what I have seen, I would guess that handwriting is about the most popular hobby in all of China.

All this emphasis on the hand skill had interesting repercussions for me as a foreign teacher. First, almost all of the students wrote exactly alike. I have been teaching for many years, and I have developed the ability to recognize students' handwriting in case one of them forgets to put his name on his paper. Presently, I have one hundred and ten students in a class, and each one writes with a distinctive flair. Not so in China. I couldn't tell one student's handwriting from another, and when they forgot to put their names on their papers, as university students around the world sometimes do, I had no way to know to whom to give the credit.

The other problem with handwriting that adheres to a standard form is that they couldn't read mine. No need writing the lecture notes on the board. The students couldn't read them. I must admit that I have a distinctive style, and I don't always color within the lines; but in my native land, it isn't all that disturbing. Students can still decode it.

But with the Chinese students, any variation of the form caused them great problems, and they were often too gracious to tell me about it.

Chinese Chess

My student Jack won the university-wide Chinese chess tournament. That is quite a feat for a foreign language student playing against all those math and physics majors.

I wasn't surprised. Jack is a bright fellow. He wasn't the best English student I had. He struggled with pronunciation, but he was bold enough to spend time with me and force himself to speak. Thus, he improved. His writing improved as well once he saw that writing is just a matter of applying logic to words.

Jack has as much analytic ability as any student I have ever taught. As a part of our American culture study, I taught the students the game of tic-tac-toe. I chose Jack as my opponent for the demonstration. Bad move! He beat me every time. I had one of those games from Cracker Barrel Restaurant where you jump the golf tees trying to leave only one. Jack mastered it on his third attempt.

With that analytic mind, Jack is a natural for Chinese chess, a game that looks enough like international chess to recognize that they are in the same family but still different.

The pieces are all shaped the same, but they are distinguished by the Chinese characters printed on them. The board is constructed of squares and lines. The king himself is enclosed in a square which represents his palace which is protected by four sentries. The battlefield is separated by a river which only selected pieces can cross. The object is to capture the king.

Don't ask anymore. That is all I know. I watched Jack play all comers in the tournament, and I picked up that much. But I do know that the game is popular. Students play during their breaks. Retirees gather at People's Square and line the streets in chess games. Ditch diggers whip out the chessboard while they are relaxing on the lunch break – lots of people practicing their skill of logic.

I am curious. I wonder which came first – the international game or the Chinese game? Why are the two games similar but different?

I suppose I will never know the answers to my questions, and I doubt that I shall ever learn to play the Chinese variety.

Jack did ask me to teach him international chess, but fortunately, both of us got too busy to carry out our intentions before the student had an opportunity to wax his teacher.

Getting into the Center of the Photo

One of the most common forms of participatory activity is the sport of photograph negotiations. The rules are simple. The most important person is in the center of the photo. Of course that seems logical both from a cultural and an artistic view. It's easy to tell who is important – just find the person in the middle. When the photos come out in the newspaper or are passed around at family reunions or are filed away for historical records, it is good to be able to see immediately who among the group had won the title of "Most Important."

But the process of selecting the appropriate person to get into the center of the photo is rather similar to an aerobics workout. When you are the uninitiated foreigner, you find yourself being pushed to the center regardless of the circumstance, but as you watch the ritual negotiations for the remaining positions, you suddenly realize that you shouldn't have taken the spot without some resistance. After that, you engage in the sport as vigorously as everyone else.

Someone in the crowd says, "Let's take a photo," and the camera comes out. Immediately, everyone gets into the act, crowding and pushing. "You must be here," they all tell you, but you shouldn't agree.

"Oh, no, I could never think of being in the middle," you must respond. "That place is for you," and you push back. Now, the contest is on. Although there is no clock on the field, there is a requisite time for the pushing and shoving and arguing before someone acquiesces and accepts the position of honor. The photo is shot; the group is reconstructed, and it's time for the second round of negotiations. The game continues until everyone has been put into proper places and the event has been duly recorded for posterity.

I must confess that I enjoy the sport. It is more physical than golf and more competitive than tennis, but not as vicious as football.

My only problem was that I never knew who won and who lost. They never explained that to me. When I was the most aggressive and managed to nail down a spot on the side, I thought I had won until I inspected the photo later. I noticed that the person in the center always has the look of a winner.

Computers on Hand Carts

Paradox! Your home is China.

Here comes the peasant, trudging down the street, straining at every step – with a bamboo pull rod under each arm – tugging his heavy load to its destination.

The cart itself could date back to earliest inventions – a box made out of bamboo sticks woven together with reeds and mounted on a steel axle threaded through two steel wheels.

What is the load the man delivers today? Stones to be used to build a fortress against the advancing hordes? Topsoil to be scattered over rocks deep enough to grow rice in every available spot? Human waste to be used as fertilizer?

No, today the load on the handcart towed by the stone-faced peasant is a black and white box with the words "Gateway 2000" stamped in plain sight.

Welcome to China! The paradoxes! The contradictions! The first century and the twenty-first century walking hand in hand with all centuries in between lined up to form the background.

You can see this everywhere! On one side of the road, one hundred men are digging a basement using primitive grubbing hoes and carrying the soil away in buckets carried on the shoulder hitch bamboo stick. On the other side of the street, one man digs a basement operating a bulldozer with state of the art control panels.

Don't ask why because I don't know why. Economic feasibility? Utilization of labor? Tradition? But this is the way it is!

I would really like to know more about these paradoxes! I would like to find some way to get inside their hearts and find out how people feel about it.

What does that handcart man think about the pick-up truck which just whizzed by throwing gravel and dust in his face?

What do the diggers with grubbing hoes think when they take a breather, lean on their tools, and stare across at the tractor carrying more soil in one bite than they can carry in a day? Why is one man digging with a hoe while another digs with the tractor?

I don't know the answers to these questions, but I do know that someone on our street is getting a new computer – one of the best.

Momma, How Old am I?

I suppose I had always known that there are two calendars in the world – the Western calendar and the Chinese calendar. Although I was aware of the fact, it never made much of an impression on me until I arrived in China and met people who struggled with the simple question of "How old are you?"

To our students and friends, that question is not as easy as it may sound. To answer, they first have to ask another question. By which calendar are we tabulating? When they get that resolved, they still have the burden of calculation. By the time we get to an answer, "How old are you?" becomes a question demanding skills of higher mathematics.

Although the years of the two calendars are similar in length, there is enough variation to make a difference in one's age. To complicate it further, many of our friends were born during the time of the Culture Revolution when vital records such as birth dates were not a high priority. Some people don't have any idea of which year they were born, whether it's Chinese year or Western year. Not only that, but babies in China are a year old at birth because they count the time in the womb. As you can see, asking a person his age is not the best place to start a conversation.

I decided that I wanted to know more about Chinese history, so I asked. I invited the history majors over to the apartment, and I bombarded them with what I thought were good questions – thoughtful questions – meaningful questions – the kind of questions which history teachers love – questions of dates and events.

When was the Great Wall built?

How many dynasties have there been in Chinese history?

When was this book written?

When did this particular general live?

Those history majors sat and stared at me as if they were baffled. They didn't know the answers. I was disappointed. Surely they are better educated than that. This is basic knowledge I am asking about.

The next time the history majors came, they brought me a message from their professor. My asking the kinds of questions I asked demonstrated that I don't know much about Chinese history.

I wasn't offended because he is right. I was trying to see China through a Westerner's eyes – exact times and elapsed years. That's the way we study history.

But operating with the two calendars, Chinese scholars just can't be that precise, so the philosophy of historical study takes a new dimension. The details of the event are more important than the date of the event.

In the same spirit of time, life is more important than birthdays.

Tiananmen Square Ten Years Later

Annie dropped by the apartment to ask us some questions about another class.

"Dr. Schimmels, are you in trouble?" she asked with some concern in her voice. "I tried to come see you earlier today, but there is a guard at the door who is checking everyone coming into the building."

We were shocked by the news. We had been at the university almost all year with complete freedom for both us and our guests. We came and went without any feeling of restrictions whatsoever. Why did we get this new wave of security at this time of year?

Then we remembered to check the calendar – June 4, 1999 — the tenth anniversary of Tiananmen Square. We had forgotten all about it, and the students were completely oblivious to any significance of the date at all. They sensed a tension among the officials, and they noticed the additional security, but they had no clue as to why.

Although we weren't dedicated news watchers or paper readers, apparently, the special day drew little media attention. Interestingly enough, Tiananmen Square itself was closed for repairs during the weeks before, during and after the anniversary date.

I was intrigued by the students' lack of awareness about that event in their own recent history when they were so conversant about events in other parts of the world. The most obvious explanation is that all of us tend to put little importance on those events just before or early in our lives. I get upset because American students don't know the details of President Kennedy's assassination until I realize that they weren't even born at the time. Our university students last year were third graders at the time of the Tiananmen Square event, more interested in hopscotch and tag than in demonstrations and conflicts.

Another explanation for their not remembering might be that certain events in some countries are more newsworthy in other places than they are at home. Before you translate that statement as a criticism of Chinese reporting, let me assure you that it happens in many different places. Our students didn't know that it was the tenth anniversary of Tiananmen Square, but I didn't know that the United States is millions of dollars behind in United Nations payments until those same students told me.

Nine Cases
of Gifts

Most of what we took to China, we left there – books, videos, teaching supplies, snack foods (for homesick moments), and even our clothes which didn't fit after our year of rice and green tea diet.

But just because we left it there doesn't mean that we came home empty-handed. We brought home as many cases as we took, but this time they were filled with Chinese treasures. And we didn't buy a thing.

Nine cases of gifts! Gifts from our students; gifts from faculty members with whom we had worked and helped; gifts from university officials in appreciation of our services; gifts from community people we had met; gifts from schools where we had spoken; and even a gift that we received from two strangers on the street on Christmas night when we went out walking in an attempt to fight some feelings of homesickness.

Silk ties, woodcarvings, music boxes, memory books and photo albums filled by our students, fans, scented bookmarks, Chinese calligraphy and a painting worth several hundred dollars.

We now have those gifts decorating our house and our office - readily available for a quick glance and a quick memory.

Every gift is valuable to us in its own right, but every gift has a story behind it which makes it priceless.

Who are these Chinese people? What are they like? How do they think? The best answer I can give you is: nine cases of gifts! If you really want to know who the Chinese are, stop by and admire just one of those presents. I warn you! If I catch you even sneaking a peek, I'll tell you the story behind it. Then maybe you will begin to understand why we love the people so much.

Kelly's Bible

In 1990, we went to China for a summer teaching excursion. One of our students, who was herself a young college English teacher, came to our apartment one night.

She wanted to talk to me, but she wanted to go outside for the conversation. She suspected that we might have bugs, the kind of bugs that listened in on private conversations.

As we walked along in the semi-dark into places where we were confident that we were alone, she poured her heart out. She had heard of God. She liked what she had heard, but she didn't know enough to know what to think. She had heard of a book called the Bible which told of God. If we had such a book with us, could she borrow it in order to read for herself?

I promised her even better. I would give her a Bible for her very own. Unfortunately, it was in English which she could read only slowly because it was her foreign language.

Back in the apartment, we spoke cheerfully of other matters (loudly enough to confuse the bugs) while we wrapped the Bible in several layers of paper so she could secretly steal away to her home during the night. It occurred to me that I had an added duty. I needed to give her some direction. The book is too big, too complex, and too multi-dimensional for any person to make it through cover to cover without some help, particularly a person coming at it from a second language position. On the spur of the moment, I made a list of fifteen chapters which I thought might move her from zero knowledge to sufficient insights into the character of God.

Before you judge me, let me give you the same assignment. Under these conditions, which chapters would you give her? Isn't this a fun exam?

On July 2, 1999, our student and friend Kelly, another young college English teacher, was in our home helping us pack to return to the United States after our year in China. We decided to present her with one of our Bibles. She clasped it with both hands; she cried; she hugged us; she kissed her Bible, and then she excused herself to go running out of the apartment to show everybody her new prized possession. She stopped people in the streets to show them; she went to the English office to show all the other teachers; she went to the communist party secretary's office to share the good news with her. For the rest of the days we were there, Kelly carried her Bible everywhere she went. She was even carrying it when we made the final group picture.

Do you see the difference in ten years? I can't explain it, but it is there. Ten years ago people were in China sowing seeds. Now people are in China watering those seeds. Changes have come in those ten years, and the only explanation I have is that God is at work.

One thing hasn't changed, though. Kelly still needed for me to make a list of those fifteen chapters she should read.

Seeing Us Off

Our most unforgettable memory of our year in China? That's easy. Two hundred and fifty students lining the walk as we passed through on our way to the taxi which would take us to the airport for the flight home.

Seeing people off is a Chinese custom. When you go to their house for supper, they walk you halfway home at the conclusion of the evening. When a friend or a classmate catches a train for a weekend at home, at least two other friends will come along for the "Seeing Off" ceremony.

We knew about the custom, but we weren't really expecting too much ceremony. We had reached out to our students as best as we knew how, but we are foreigners in their homeland. We had established friendships, but all the while we had in the backs of our minds that we were going home when it was all over. Zhejiang Normal University was a good place for us, but it was not home; and when our time there was finished, we would go home.

We were scheduled to fly from Shanghai on the Fourth of July – Mary's birthday, and Independence Day for the U.S., but because we were finished with our classes, we decided to go from Jinhua to Shanghai on the first of July. We just didn't bother to explain this to anyone. When they asked when we were leaving, we answered, "July Fourth," and dropped the point.

Besides, the students were in the midst of final exams. They were spending all their waking hours studying and all their other hours tied into knots of anxiety. They didn't need an additional burden of seeing off the foreign teachers. For the second besides, we were scheduled to leave at 6:00 a.m. when university students all over the world should still be in bed. We had convinced ourselves that we would just slip out without disturbing anyone.

It didn't work that way. When we walked out into the early morning mist, 250 students were waiting for us. Taking a page from the movie, *Dead Poet's Society*, they had climbed up on the retaining wall for another perspective, and they were holding a computer-produced banner which read, "O Captain, My Captain."

We walked through those laughing and crying and applauding students on our way to the car.

That's our memory of our China. That's our evaluation of how the year went. That's our description of what kind of people the Chinese are.

Appendix A

A Word to Universities Interested in a Partnership with Cooperative Studies

Cooperative Studies is dedicated to assisting public universities outside of North America by placing academicians and professionals on their faculties. The goal of CS is to help provide academic programs which promote cross-cultural understanding, an appreciation for the richness of each culture and a moral, ethical and philosophical foundation for education.

Cooperative Studies lecturers emphasize the unique contributions which political, social, philosophical and religious values have had on their particular discipline. We are committed to the principle that truly good people make for a good society. Thus we seek to encourage both academic and ethical development among students. We insist on the highest level of moral and ethical behavior in the professors we provide, both in their teaching and professional lives as well as in their personal lives and interaction within the academic community. CS has worked for several years with universities in China, as well as in Ukraine, Russia, Vietnam and Bangladesh.

Cooperative Studies is ready to consider a partnership with accredited, state-recognized universities and institutions of higher education. We work only with accredited universities and medical schools, primarily those which are state-sponsored. CS does not work with religious colleges and universities.

CS recruits lecturers across the entire spectrum of academic disciplines. CS Teaching Fellows possess high standards of scholarship and academic excellence, an outstanding record of classroom instruction and a commitment to intercultural global understanding.

Our goal is to combine educational developments around the world with the unique needs and goals of each nation in order to improve the overall quality of curriculum and education without sacrificing the national, ethnic, or social distinctives of that society.

A sound international partnership program can help provide a balanced university education in which the student becomes knowledgeable in a wide range of ideas which have shaped the historical, literary, linguistic, and philosophical values of civilization. It sharpens the social, critical, analytical and evaluative skills of the students.

For more information on establishing a university partnership with Cooperative Studies, you are invited to contact:

Cooperative Studies
P.O. Box 12830
Overland Park, KS 66282-2830
Phone: 913-962-9961 Fax: 913-962-9388
Email: edu@coopstudies.org
Web site: www.coopstudies.org

Appendix B
Academicians and Professionals Interested in Teaching Positions

*I*magine that your teaching could make a difference in the world....

Every single day. Many academicians have found the experience of teaching overseas is life-changing. If you would like to broaden your world by teaching in China or some other nation, you are encouraged to apply to Cooperative Studies.

Dr. Charles Malik, who taught at American University in Beirut, as well as Dartmouth and Harvard, and was president of the United Nations General Assembly and Security Council, said,

"At the heart of all the problems facing Western civilization—the general nervousness and restlessness, the dearth of grace and beauty and quiet and peace of soul, the manifold blemishes and perversions of personal character; problems of the family and of social relations in general, problems of economics and politics, problems of the media, problems affecting the school itself and the church itself, problems in the international order—at the heart of the crisis in Western civilization

lies the state of the mind and the spirit in the universities....
Where do the leaders in these realms come from? They all
come from universities. What they are fed, intellectually, morally,
spiritually, personally, in the fifteen or twenty years they spend in
the school and university, is the decisive question. It is there that
the foundations of character and mind and outlook and convic-
tion and attitude and spirit are laid...."(Malik, *The Two Tasks*, 30).

Malik declared,"The university is a clear-cut fulcrum with
which to move the world....Change the university and you
change the world" (*A Christian Critique of the University*, 100-101).

Cooperative Studies is seeking academicians and professionals who are interested in teaching as members of public university faculties outside of North America and the UK. Consider a
teaching assignment with Cooperative Studies, a professional
academic organization which provides faculty for public universities overseas. CS has invitations from scores of universities
around the world.

CS provides each faculty member with...
> The teaching opportunity of a lifetime
> A contract to serve on the faculty of an overseas
>   secular university
> Training and orientation for your assignment
> Ongoing assistance in raising and sustaining financial
>   support
> Experienced support staff
> Arbitration with the university in problem situations

TESTIMONIALS FROM OVERSEAS CS FACULTY MEMBERS

Dr. Scott Higgins, business professor, Zheijiang University, China "Your life is never the same after serving overseas."

Mrs. Jeanelle Higgins, ESL professor, Zheijiang University, China "CS raises the educational standard high and promotes trust between the university, the professor and the students."

Dr. Roger Ford, Hanoi School of Business, Hanoi, Vietnam, "Since joining CS, I have engaged 100% of my skills and energy 100% of the time - in a place where it really matters. Universities in the West are typically filled with bored students and professors who wonder if their lives have significance. Boredom does not exist here – and every day is significant.... The CS program is exhilarating, but also exhausting - and not for everybody!"

CS is accepting applications from persons in...
> Engineering Sciences
> Social Sciences
> Humanities
> Medicine
> Education
> Religion
> Natural Sciences
> Business & Management
> Law
> Other academic disciplines

For more information you are invited to contact:
Dr. Daryl McCarthy, Executive Director
> Cooperative Studies
> P.O. Box 12830
> Overland Park, KS 66282-2830
> Phone: 913-962-9961 Fax: 913-962-9388
> Email: edu@coopstudies.org
> Web site: www.coopstudies.org

REQUEST FOR INFORMATION

Please copy or detach and mail this form to:
Cooperative Studies
P.O. Box 12830
Overland Park, KS 66282-2830
Phone: 913-962-9961 Fax: 913-962-9388

I would consider teaching overseas with CS for:
_____More than one year
_____One to two semesters

My next sabbatical is_____

_____Please send me an application and more information
on an overseas teaching position.

Name _____

Address_____

City_____ State/Province _____

Zip/Postal Code _____Country_____

Home Phone: _____
Office Phone: _____
Fax: _____
Email address:

_____

Highest degree earned and field of study :

_____